REMEMBER ME

*Achievements of Mixed Race
People, Past and Present*

Asher & Martin Hoyles

Hansib Publications Ltd
& Ethos Publishing

First published in 1999 by
Hansib Publications Limited & Ethos Publishing
Tower House, 141-149 Fonthill Road, London N4 3HF, England

© Asher & Martin Hoyles

ISBN 1 870518 62 4

Cover designed by Stefan Brazzo
Production and origination by Hansib Publications Ltd
Printed and bound in Great Britain by Martins the Printers,
Berwick upon Tweed

DEDICATION

This book is dedicated to our daughter Rosa Aretha Hoyles.
We thank her for her cooperation while writing it.

ACKNOWLEDGEMENTS

We would like to thank all those who agreed to be interviewed for the book and also the following for their invaluable help in producing it: Arif Ali, Yasmin Alibhai-Brown, David A. Bailey, Clement Cooper, Gary Douglas, Charles Engmann, Margaret Hoyles, Jayne Ifekwunigwe, The Lennon Family, Jonathan Manley, Norma Pitfield, Phil Vasili.

PICTURE CREDITS

CONTENTS

REMEMBER ME

INTRODUCTION

There is one race - the human race. Recent archaeological evidence suggests that this human race began life in Africa and spread out from there to the rest of the world. But for much of our recent history many people have believed in dividing the world into different races. Particularly because of slavery and the colonisation of Africa, theories were invented to justify treating some human beings differently because of the colour of their skin.

Today scientists no longer accept the idea of race as a *biological* fact. Genetically there are more differences between the different peoples of Africa than between Africans and non-Africans. Nevertheless race is still a *social* and *political* fact. Racism is still a common experience for many people, usually based on the colour of their skin.

Although biologically we are all multiracial, mixed relationships have historically often been viewed with hostility. In the nineteenth century, in particular, they were thought to dilute the so-called purity of the race, leading to disease, early death and eventual extinction. In Nazi Germany mixed-race people were persecuted and many were sterilized or killed in concentration camps. In Australia mixed-race children were often forcibly removed from their Aboriginal mothers in order to try and make them 'disappear' in the white population.

In the USA most states banned interracial marriages. The law was enacted as early as 1661 in Maryland. In 1958 Mildred Jeter, a black Native American woman, married Perry Loving, a white man, in the state of Virginia. The following year they were sentenced to one year in prison. As late as 1967, when the Supreme Court finally made the ban illegal, these laws still existed

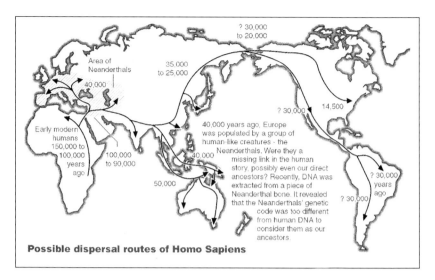

? 30,000
to 20,000

Area of
Neanderthals

35,000
to 25,000

40,000

14,500

? 30,000

Early modern
humans
150,000 to
100,000
years
ago

100,000
to 90,000

40,000

40,000 years ago, Europe
was populated by a group of
human-like creatures - the
Neanderthals. Were they a
missing link in the human
story, possibly even our direct
ancestors? Recently, DNA was
extracted from a piece of
Neanderthal bone. It revealed
that the Neanderthals' genetic
code was too different
from human DNA to
consider them as our
ancestors.

50,000

? 30,000

? 30,000
years
ago

Possible dispersal routes of Homo Sapiens

in one-third of the states. Similar laws were also proposed for Britain in the 1920s.

At the other extreme Josephine Schuyler believed that mixed marriages would produce *superior* people. She was a white Texan heiress who married a famous black journalist, George Schuyler. Their daughter Philippa, able to read and write at the age of two, a pianist at four and a composer at five, was often compared to Mozart. She became an international performer and a role model for many in America's black communities. However her mother's intense pressure on Philippa to succeed and the racism in the USA led to a severe identity crisis, as Philippa explains: 'I am a beauty - but I'm half-colored so I'm not accepted anyplace. I'm always destined to be an outsider, never, never *part* of anything. I hate my country and no one wants me in any other. I am emotionally part of nothing and that will always be my destiny.'

'I was mixed race; Louise Buttercup was white, my father was African. Yet I wasn't simply a bringing together of opposites. I was me. Distinct. A race apart.' Lucinda Roy *Lady Moses* 1998

Names for people of mixed parents were offensive. Mulatto, from the Portuguese word for a young mule, was used in the United States and West Indies. It expressed the common view of many racists that mixed-race people would become infertile like the mule. Metis, meaning a mongrel dog, was the French term;

mestizo the Spanish and Portuguese word; mixed-breed and half breed were common in Britain; while today half-caste is still to be heard.

Categories were devised to describe mixed-race people: mulatto for half black, quadroon for a quarter black, octoroon for an eighth black, and so on. In Spanish there are 128 words for different combinations of mixed races. In Brazil there were 492 different categories: the lighter the skin the higher the status. This grading by skin colour is sometimes called pigmentocracy.

In *The Multiracial Experience* (1996) Maria Root records a survey she conducted in a junior college in Honolulu, Hawaii, 'a geographic location heralded for its racial blending'. She compiled a list of about 30 different words used for someone who is racially mixed: 'Many of the references were to animals, and most were labels used to refer to dogs.'

The grading of skin colour is still with us today. But as Maud Sulter points out in *The Privilege of the Fairskinned*, it depends on the context whether light skin is privileged. She compares 'down here' in London to 'up there' in Scotland:

> *Down here*
> *privilege relates to*
> *How light skin gets you this*
> *light skin gets you that*
>
> *No doubt that's true*
> *but that's down here*
>
> *Up there*
> *If you're the only black*
> *in the neighbourhood*
> *it makes no difference*
>
> *Nigger Darkie Paki*
> *all means the same to them*
>
> *Privilege,*
> *being relative,*
> *isn't a constructive*
> *measure of oppression.*

In racist societies, with their view that one drop of black blood makes a person black, mixed-race people are usually viewed as black, in other words not white. Consequently most mixed-race people in Britain and America have considered themselves black and this has been an important political position. Jon Michael Spencer, from the USA, sees it as a survival strategy: 'Blacks are concerned that mixed-race children who are raised as something other than black are being denied the opportunity to learn the survival skills that come with being raised as black, and that one day these children may be traumatized when they learn that society sees them as black.'

Similarly Lenny Kravitz, the American rock star, says: 'You don't have to deny the White side of you if you're mixed. Accept the blessing of having the advantage of two cultures, but understand that you are Black. In this world, if you have one spot of Black blood, you are *Black*.'

Herb Jeffries, the American singer and movie star of the 1940s and 1950s, was light-skinned enough to pass and was advised to present himself as a Spaniard of Latin American origin in order to further his career. Jeffries refused, quoting the one-drop rule: 'I'd always heard that if you had *any* Negro blood you were a Negro and that was that. Then it can't be such inferior blood, can it? If you had a black paint that was so powerful that two drops of it would color a bucket of white, that'd be the most potent paint in the world, wouldn't it? So if Negro blood is as strong as all that it must be pretty good - maybe I'd better find out where I can get some more of it.'

The American writer Lisa Jones writes: 'My mother is white. And I, as you may or may not have figured out, am black. This is how I choose to define myself and this is how America chooses to define me. I have no regrets about my racial classification other than to lament, off and on, that classification exists period.' Her Jewish mother, who had been disowned by her parents for 'marrying black', knew that her two daughters 'needed black female relatives and role models, and she made sure that these ties were in place'. As Lisa Jones says: 'It was my (white) mother who raised me to think politically about being a black woman.'

Generally mixed-race people in the USA have been more at home in black communities. Black people have been more accepting of mixed relationships. A Gallup Poll in 1972 showed

25% of whites approving interracial marriage and 58% of blacks. In 1983 the figures were 43% for whites and 71% for blacks.

'I identify as Black for the purposes of census-taking or any other purpose, but I am not ashamed of my non-Black ancestry. I should be allowed to be who I am and so should everyone else.' Carol Camper *Miscegenation Blues: Voices of Mixed Race Women* 1994

Carol Camper, from Canada, writes that she was not confused as a child about race because she did not know her race at all. She is mixed black, white and native American, but was adopted by a white family. Not until she was ten years old and read some books about anthropology did she discover information about racial mixing: 'For the first time I had an idea of how to explain myself to myself. I went to the mirror and made my own assessment of what I was and then confronted my adoptive mother. "What am I, Mum? Am I part white and part Black?" "Yes" the reply came, along with sketchy information about a Black birth mother. I thought that my Black mother may have had non-Black ancestry as well, because of my light skin. I found out many years later that she has First Nations' ancestry and that this is very common. My mother's family are descendants of American slaves (escapees via the Underground Railroad) from the Carolinas who had mixed with Native people.'

Another Canadian, Heather Green, also had to struggle to find her African heritage. Her mother was English and her father Jamaican, but she was brought up by her mother and white stepfather. She did not learn about her father until she was eighteen years old. It was reading about Bob Marley that taught her about her roots: 'The day I read that Bob Marley was of *African and European* parentage, was the day I began to lay down my burden of being mixed with European blood and feeling "unauthentically" Black - "unauthentically" African. I decided that I would burn the whip with which I beat myself for not being pure enough. I stopped biting my tongue every time I wanted and *needed* to say, "As a Black woman... As an African woman..."'

There may now be coming a time in which the various heritages of mixed-race people can all be valued and celebrated. A hundred years ago W. E. B. Du Bois expressed this hope in *The Souls of Black Folk*: 'The history of the American Negro is the history of this strife - this longing to attain self-conscious manhood, to merge his double self into a better and truer self. In this merging he wishes neither of the older selves to be lost. He would not Africanize America, for America has too much to teach the world and Africa. He would not bleach his Negro soul in a flood of white Americanism, for he knows that Negro blood has a message for the world. He simply wishes to make it possible for a man to be both a Negro and an American, without being cursed and spit upon by his fellows, without having the doors of Opportunity closed roughly in his face.'

South African society was built on the idea of the separation of people of different colour. Even today, with the dismantling of apartheid, it was reported in *The Guardian* (26 November 1997) that a white member of a Christian church in Port Elizabeth said: 'I have to tell you the truth: if my daughter came in with a black boyfriend I'd hit the roof. I'm a strong Christian, but if the choice was between her marrying a black Christian or a white atheist, I wouldn't like to tell you which way I'd go. No I will tell you: I'd hope she married the white guy and then tried to convert him.'

This is typical of the position that views mixed relationships with horror. It has led to the idea that they are bound to be a problem, the partners are more likely to split up and the children will be confused, belonging to neither one culture nor the other. In *Negroes in Britain* (1947), for example, K. L. Little writes of mixed-race people in Bute Town, Cardiff, (where Shirley Bassey was born): 'They lack on the one hand the cultural and national pride upon which many of their fathers at the worst can fall back, and on the other they fail to gain any compensatory ties in the society of the land in which they were born. Many of their actions are negative rather than positive; their behaviour is accounted unreliable; and their characters sometimes appear shiftless.'

There is some truth in this idea, as mixed relationships often face the pressure of racist abuse. But it is far from being the whole truth, as James McBride recognises in *The Color of Water: a Black Man's Tribute to his White Mother*, published in 1998. His mother was a Polish Jew and his father an African American minister. McBride describes the tensions in the household as his mother brought up twelve mixed-race children. After one embarrassing episode with his mother, he writes: 'I thought it would be easier if we were just one color, black or white. I didn't want to be white. My siblings had already instilled the notion of black pride in me. I would have preferred that Mommy were black. Now, as a grown man, I feel privileged to have come from two worlds. My view of the world is not merely that of a black man but of a black man with something of a Jewish soul.'

Linda Alcoff, with a Panamanian father (mixed Spanish, Indian and African) and a white Anglo-Irish mother from the United States, also describes her experience of being mixed-race as 'painful and at times confusing'. In Panama they were 'of the appropriately valued lighter type', but when they moved to Florida they were referred to as her mother's 'Latin daughters' and could 'occupy white identity only precariously'. In *Mestizo Identity* (a chapter in Naomi Zack's *American Mixed Race*) Alcoff writes: 'Without a social recognition of mixed identity, the mixed-race person is told to choose one or another perspective.'

Alcoff does, however, see a very positive role for mixed-race people: 'The mixed person is a traveller often within her own home or neighbourhood, translating and negotiating the diversity of meanings, practices, and forms of life. This vision provides a positive alternative to the mixed-race person's usual representation as lack or as the tragically alienated figure.'

'It may be, then, that the undoing of racial classification will come not by initiating a new classification, which will only give Americans the impression that mixed-race people can be neatly classified, but by our increased recognition that there are millions of people who cannot be put into neat categories.' Jon Michael Spencer *The New Colored People: The Mixed-Race Movement in America* 1997

Why should mixed-race people have to wait until later life to see the benefits of belonging to more than one culture? It should be possible to learn this as children. This is why education is so important, as Francis Wardle points out in *Multicultural Education* (in *The Multiracial Experience* edited by Maria Root): 'Multicultural education that recognizes and supports biracial children is based on two basic assumptions. The first is that biracial children have the inalienable right to their true identity. They need their entire heritage to be recognized and supported. And they need to be viewed as normal, well-adjusted individuals. Second, schools and professionals have an obligation to support, nurture, and celebrate biracial children, their families, and history.'

This is also the view of Nila Gupta whose father is Indian and her mother French Canadian. Writing in *Miscegenation Blues*, she has a vision of the future: 'I think I can envision that what would make interracial marriages healthy, would be if people were racially conscious: if they understood the history, if they did their research, if they did their learning, their growing. That would take a lot of the pain away. It could not shelter you from the larger societal context, but in terms of the family, it could give you a place of strength and empower you to go on with your life. I can envision that. It's not the fact that we're bi-racial that is problematic, it's that there is so much silence, and ignorance, and racism.'

This book, *Remember Me*, is an attempt to help this learning process. It challenges the view that being of mixed race is simply a problem. By looking at the positive achievements of mixed-race people, it shows how belonging to more than one culture and tradition can be an advantage.

Danielle Brown, aged 17, who is an actress in the British TV soap *Emmerdale* and also the sister of Mel B of the Spice Girls, acknowledged this in 1998: 'Reports last week made out I was really distraught because I don't have blonde hair and blue eyes, and that as a child I wanted straight blonde hair like my friends because I didn't want to be different. But I don't want that now, I'm really glad I've got my hair. If I could change my mum and dad to both being black or both being white I would keep them just the way they are. Even though having a black dad and a white mum has caused me and Mel hassle, it's all been worth it.'

The poet Bernardine Evaristo, born to a Nigerian father and English mother, symbolizes her mixed heritage in her poem *Bedtime Story* by referring to her parents' musical tastes. For Christmas she was given jazz and classical records: the saxophonist John Coltrane from her father and Bach from her mother:

> *My mother was a teacher.*
> *My father, a carpenter.*
> *They were musicians.*
> *They loved music.*
> *He was tall.*

He was slim
with large brown eyes
and a velvet brown skin.
He played jazz:
'Slim & His Quartet'.
She played piano.
She played Bach -
in the living room.

Henry Louis Gates also wants the best of both worlds. Married to a white woman, he addresses his memoirs *Colored People* to his two young daughters: 'I want to be black, to know black, to luxuriate in whatever I might be calling blackness at any particular time - but to do so in order to come out the other side, to experience a humanity that is neither colorless nor reducible to color. Bach *and* James Brown. Sushi *and* fried catfish.'

Similarly Bob Purkiss of the TUC is proud of his English roots and his African American heritage, and he also sees himself as Jamaican. He says: 'We must make sure that mixed-race families are made more visible so that the growing number of mixed-race children do not have to face a society which sweeps their experiences under the carpet.'

One positive achievement was that of the French author Alexandre Dumas, who wrote *The Three Musketeers* and *The Count of Monte Cristo*. In 1847 he wrote the following letter to a Democrat from the southern states of America: 'Sir, My mother was a Negro and I am not ashamed to confess that my person makes open declaration of my lineage. I am anxious to visit your country. One thing deters me. I am told that my African blood will subject me to inconvenience in your country, and that I may even be taken and sold as a slave, according to existing laws.'

Another was that of Alexander Pushkin, the most famous Russian poet. He was proud of his mother's grandfather, who was the son of an Abyssinian prince, sent to Constantinople as a hostage. His name was Abram Petrovich Hannibal and he died, aged 92, in 1781.

The issue of mixed heritage was also important to the composer Samuel Taylor-Coleridge. He was convinced that some of his heroes, such as Beethoven and Robert Browning, 'had coloured blood in their veins'.

'No separate history of people of mixed black and white parentage has been written. In this sense, as a group they have no past, and no heroes or heroines with whom to identify.' Barbara Tizard and Ann Phoenix *Black, White or Mixed Race* 1993

Alexander Pushkin by Egor Geitman

This book remembers many mixed-race figures in history, who have often been forgotten. It deals mainly with people who had one white parent and one of African origin, though there are clearly many other kinds of mixture which need to be celebrated.

The ethnic mix of Tiger Woods, for example, includes African American, Chinese, Thai, Caucasian and Native American. In 1997, at the age of 21, he became the youngest player ever to win the Masters golf tournament. When he was a child, his father identified himself and his son as African American, but later Tiger invented the term 'Cablinasian' (**Ca**ucasian, **Bl**ack, **In**dian, **Asian**) to describe his mixed heritage.

By the middle of the eighteenth century there were at least 10,000 black people in Britain, most of them brought back as slaves or servants by plantation owners from the West Indies. Some of them were mixed-race. White planters in the West Indies, for example, often used to send their mixed-race children to Britain for their education. Many of the slaves and servants who ended up in Britain freed themselves by running away and were active in the anti-slavery movement. Many also married local white women.

One of these was Dr Johnson's famous black servant, Francis Barber, who was born in Jamaica. He eventually married an English woman and settled in Lichfield, Staffordshire. Another was Ukawsaw Gronniosaw, grandson of a king from Nigeria, who was kidnapped by slave-traders at the age of fifteen. After he was freed by his master, he served in the British Army and then married a weaver called Betty, a poor English widow with a child. They had three children altogether, though it is not known what happened to them.

Olaudah Equiano also came from Nigeria. He was the first political leader of Britain's black community. He campaigned all round the country against the slave-trade and his memoirs were published as a book. He married a white woman from Ely, called Susan Cullen, and they had two daughters, though one died at the age of four. Two hundred years ago he advocated mixed marriages: 'Why not establish intermarriages at home, and in our Colonies? and encourage open, free and generous love, upon Nature's own wide and extensive plan, subservient only to moral rectitude, without distinction of the colour of a skin?'

Joseph Emidy, from Guinea, was taken by Portuguese slavers to Brazil where his musical talent was spotted by Jesuit priests who sent him to Lisbon. In 1795 he was kidnapped by the British Navy and, after spending five years playing the hornpipe for the sailors' entertainment on board the ship *Indefatigable*, he eventually landed in Falmouth, Cornwall, at the age of 24. Here he set up as a composer, teacher and performer He married a local woman called Jenefer Hutchins and had six children. Their second child, Thomas, born in 1805, was a musician like his father.

By the end of the nineteenth century, however, there were few black people living in Britain, except for sailors who had settled in ports such as Cardiff, Liverpool and London. The descendants of the black slaves and servants had largely disappeared through intermarriage with white people. Most were poor and the records of their lives have been lost. Thousands of British families, however, if they could trace their roots, would find that they have an African ancestor.

'Mixed Race is not recognized as an identity or form of culture by those individuals - the majority - who believe that they are racially pure.' Naomi Zack *American Mixed Race* 1995

Now, at the millennium, hundreds of thousands of people in Britain are in mixed relationships. A recent survey by the Policy Studies Institute shows that 40% of black children have one white parent. Half of all British-born black men and a third of their female counterparts have a white partner.

Similarly in the USA, the Bureau of the Census in 1992 forecast that by the year 2050 the majority of Americans will no longer be white. One major cause is mixed-race babies which have increased

26 times more than any other measured group. In 1968, 72% of Americans disapproved of interracial marriage, but by 1991 this was down to 42%, while 48% approved.

The number of mixed-race children is set to increase greatly in the next decade. Hopefully this book will start to put the record straight regarding their history and tradition, and help give them more choice as to how they see their identity.

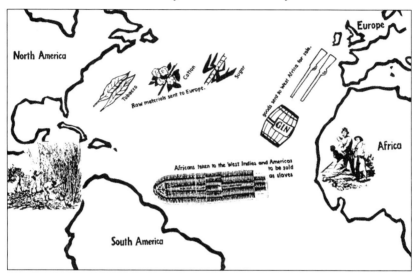

The 'Triangular Trade'

The twenty historical figures presented here span the last two and a half centuries. The connecting thread between them all is the slave-trade and the African diaspora, the dispersal of people from the African continent to the four corners of the world. The particular focus of the book is on the USA, the Caribbean and Britain, but there are clearly many similar stories to be told from other parts of the world.

The ten contemporary people are all from Britain - from England, Scotland and Wales. They represent major achievements in politics and the arts, though many other fields of activity could have been chosen. We hope they will provide inspiration and encouragement to all who read the book.

PART ONE

Contemporary Biographies

CLEO LAINE

Cleo Laine is an internationally famous jazz singer and actress.

She was born in October 1927 in Clarence Street in Southall, Middlesex, and was given the name Clementina Dinah. Her mother, Minnie Blanche, was English, born and brought up in Swindon, and her father's name was Alexander Sylvan Campbell. He came from Jamaica and served as a soldier in the 1914-18 war. Cleo sees her mother as an early feminist, making up her own mind about who to marry and not caring about society's prejudices.

Both her parents worked selling things from door to door. When Cleo was born, her mother likened her to a 'skinned rabbit - long and thin and hairless'! Her elder sister was called Sylvia and her younger brother's name was Alec.

Cleo caught many childhood diseases, including pneumonia, which at that time meant almost certain death for a young child. However her mother nursed her in hospital and Cleo survived. She later recovered also from diphtheria and bronchitis, and twice nearly lost her sight in accidents at home.

As a child Cleo loved adventures. She liked playing with boys as she believed they did more interesting things than girls and she has memories of getting up to all kinds of mischief. Once a boy put her finger through a big wooden clothes wringer in the garden and she had to have stitches in it.

Cleo felt positive about both sides of her identity, learning about the Caribbean and seeing it as a beautiful and friendly place with wonderful food. Her father had an excellent singing voice and both parents encouraged Cleo's interest in music. Although they were not well off, she was sent to a lady called Madame De Courcey to learn to dance (ballet, tap and acrobatics) and she

also took singing and piano lessons. She wanted to dance like Fred Astaire and her role models were Ella Fitzgerald and Sarah Vaughan.

When she was three Cleo had her first opportunity to perform in public, with her sister and brother at a Southall working men's club. She was to sing a song called *Let's All Sing The Barmaid's Song*, but at the last minute had stage fright so her sister had to drag her on. It worked, and once on stage she was not to be moved and sang the song over and over again!

Although she like school at first, Cleo soon started playing truant, spending whole days in the park, on the swings and roundabouts until home time. Eventually she was discovered and the school board man came to see her parents. The headmaster caned her and this was to happen quite often, for being late or talking when she was meant to be quiet.

She liked her music teacher, Miss Owen, however, and was asked by her to sing *Shenandoah* to the music class. Cleo recalls that 'her music lessons were inventive and adventurous for those days. I was in my element, singing along like my Pa might have done without any embarrassment, just great joy in letting rip.' She was asked to sing two songs for the school concert: *The Last Rose of Summer* and *Rock a Bye Your Baby*.

As her parents moved house a lot, Cleo went to several schools. She ended up at Mellow Lane Senior School in Hayes End, west London, where she played a part in Shakespeare's *A Midsummer Night's Dream*. She also acted as an extra in the film *The Thief of Baghdad*. Singing and performing were an important part of her childhood and, although the doors of opportunity did not open for her straightaway, she remained hopeful and kept her ambitions alive by attending auditions and talent contests.

The Second World War had started and when she left school at fourteen, she had to earn a living. After being apprenticed to a hairdresser and working with a milliner, learning how to trim hats, she got a job as a librarian. It was in the library that she discovered her love of books, making up for all the books she did not read at school.

Cleo got married as a teenager and had a baby boy called Stuart. She also did her first semi-professional gig, at a Labour Party dance which took place at her old school in Hayes End. Her father came to hear her and was very proud of her performance.

Because of her determination to succeed, Cleo eventually got the opportunity to audition for the famous modern jazz band known as The Dankworth Seven. The audition took place at the 51 Club in Great Newport Street, Soho. Cleo sang three songs and, after a nervous wait, John Dankworth told her how impressed he was with her voice and that they wanted her to be their vocalist.

This gave Cleo the opportunity to develop into a famous jazz singing star. She performed all round the world, on radio and television, in cabaret and variety. Her experiences brought her into contact with stars such as Ella Fitzgerald, Quincy Jones, Frank Sinatra, Ray Charles and Dudley Moore, with whom she made an album called *Smilin' Through*. She fell in love with John Dankworth and, after divorcing her first husband, married John secretly in 1958. They had two children, Alec who became a musician and Jackie who is now an actress.

Soon after the wedding she got her first major acting role, in *Flesh to a Tiger* directed by Tony Richardson, at the famous Royal Court Theatre in west London. She played the lead as a young Jamaican woman and was congratulated by Sir Laurence Olivier after the first-night performance. At this time she also became interested in writing lyrics and poems, after reading the poetry of e. e. cummings.

In 1971 she appeared in the London revival of *Show Boat*, the great American musical. It was particularly important for her as a mixed-race woman to play the part of the mixed-race Julie, as previously only white women had played the role. It became the longest running *Show Boat* ever produced, playing 910 performances at the Adelphi Theatre.

Cleo has produced over fifty albums. One of her favourites, which she is most proud of, is *Shakespeare and all that Jazz* (1964) with some glorious settings of Shakespeare's words and sonnets. She has received many awards, including a Grammy for *Cleo at Carnegie* (1985), and was made a Dame in 1997, the first jazz singer to receive such an honour.

When she is not touring, Cleo divides her time between homes in Wavendon, in Buckinghamshire, and California. She enjoys being with her children and grandchildren and encourages them to be proud of their background. Around the house she has pictures of her grandmother in the West Indies.

Cleo believes that children should speak out for themselves and have a point of view. Along with her husband, she has pioneered the Wavendon AllPlan Music Centre, which aims to teach children all different kinds of music with the same enthusiasm that her parents passed on to her.

SHIRLEY BASSEY

Shirley Veronica Bassey is an international singing star from Wales.

She was born in Butetown, the dock area of Cardiff, known as Tiger Bay, on 8 January 1937, and was the youngest of seven children. Her father was Nigerian, a ship's fireman in the merchant navy. Her mother was a white woman from Yorkshire, called Eliza Jane Metcalfe. Shirley says of her mother: 'If my mother ever had any trouble because of marrying a West African she never told us. But somehow I have the impression her family didn't like it. Perhaps that's why she moved to Cardiff.'

When she was two, Shirley's parents were divorced and her mother was left to raise the family on National Assistance. She remembers, however, that when boats docked, black friends of her father would knock on the front door and give the kids sweets and presents.

When she was four, the family moved to nearby Splott, where she went to Moorland Road primary school. Shirley resisted racist taunts from other children by 'roughing them up a bit'. As a girl she wanted to be a nurse or a model. She was always singing, but was painfully shy: 'I used to do it under a table or in a cupboard. I'm still so shy that walking into a room can be difficult.'

Her mother said: 'Even when she was a little girl she was always singing. She used to come home at lunchtime to sweep the hall and the stairs. All her friends would stand around outside the open front door listening to her singing while she swept. I think she took after her father who was always putting on the gramophone and fooling around with the kids when he came home from sea.'

During the Second World War Shirley used to listen to the popular songs on the radio and sing along to them. While doing so she realised that she only needed to hear a tune once and she could memorise every note and phrase.

When she left school Shirley worked in a factory packing enamel goods. It was the first chance to get her name known. She said: 'I was employed wrapping bed chambers - pee pots - and I used to write my name on them and get replies from people all over the place.'

By 1953 Shirley was making a name for herself in Cardiff clubs and throughout the Welsh valleys. She finally left the factory after being offered a small part in a travelling show called *Memories of Jolson*.

In 1955 she was signed to appear in *Such is Life*, a touring show which was built around the comedian Al Read. It was here that the Bassey voice made its name and her reputation as a singing sex symbol spread round Britain. Before she was twenty she had sung in London, Paris, Monte Carlo, New York and Las Vegas. In 1957 she had her first hit, the calypso-flavoured *Banana Boat Song*. This was followed by *As I Love You* and *Kiss Me Honey Honey Kiss Me*, both entering the top ten at the same time.

As Long As He Needs Me, from the musical *Oliver*, climbed to number two in the charts and had a 30-week stay in the top 50. In 1964 she recorded the James Bond theme song *Goldfinger*, which sold more than a million copies in the USA alone, followed by *Diamonds Are Forever* and *Moonraker*.

In the 1970s Shirley recorded songs by many leading contemporary songwriters, including Stephen Sondheim, Andrew Lloyd Webber, Charles Aznavour, Jacques Brel, Harry Nilsson, Janis Ian and George Benson, and such noted lyricists as Tim Rice, Don Black, Herbert Kretzmer and Norman Newell. In 1976 she was named the Best Female Entertainer by the American Guild of Variety Artists.

In 1995 her recording for TV of *An Audience With Shirley Bassey* attracted more than ten million viewers and her 60th birthday was celebrated by a TV special, broadcast in January 1997. The highlight of recent years has been her British tours. In 1998, 120,000 people saw her live and she smashed her own record in London for the longest run by a solo artist at the Royal Festival Hall with ten sold-out shows.

Shirley has lived in Switzerland, Los Angeles, Spain and Monte Carlo, but maintains a home in the UK. She has a strict diet and

does almost daily work-outs: 'I travel with a juicer and, as soon as I get up in the morning, my assistant makes me some fresh orange, apple or pineapple juice. Then I have a coffee and some whole-wheat toast, jam and a mashed banana. After that I go to the gym for an hour. Then I stretch for half an hour, and afterwards I sit in a yoga position to do the neck exercises and roll my head.'

As well as her first daughter Sharon, she had two more children and now has four grandchildren: 'I know I haven't been a good mother - not like Sharon, who is wonderful. I sit and watch her and admire her patience. I adore the grandchildren.'

Despite her fame she still remembers her background: 'One side of me is the glamorous, romantic side. The other is still that little girl that left home at sixteen. I didn't go through my teenage years like any other teenager, with lots of boys coming round to pick you up and take you to the local dance. I missed all that. The girl offstage, Shirley Bassey offstage, sort of dreams about that, I suppose. I've always been a dreamer, and that's what helps me to do what I do on stage.'

Some of Shirley Bassey's other famous songs are *I Who Have Nothing*, *Something*, *Burning My Candle* and *Big Spender*. Her favourite jazz singer is Ella Fitzgerald and 'as for male singers, Sinatra is way out in front'. Shirley's reputation is now as great as her idol Judy Garland. She is one of Britain's most successful singing stars with more hit singles and best selling albums than any other female performer.

BOB PURKISS

Bob Purkiss is a member of the TUC Executive Committee and General Council and is a Senior Commissioner at the Commission for Racial Equality.

He was born on 11 November 1945 in Winchester and lived with his white English mother in a little village on the edge of the New Forest, where she was very active in the local Labour party. His father was an African American soldier from Arizona who left the family after the war to return to the USA.

Bob's earliest memories are of Sunday school in the Gospel Church where he sang in the church choir. He was the only black person in his primary school where he was good at sports and also came top of the class. At secondary school he took up boxing and became a school prefect. His mother experienced a great deal of racism, being the mother of a black child, but she resisted it and always encouraged Bob to do his best.

When he left school Bob joined the merchant navy and went to sea at the age of 16. At 21 he became a bosun. His first journey was to South Africa and he was one of only two black people on the ship. The captain had to explain apartheid to them, that they would be treated as 'Cape coloured' and that there would be certain places where they could not go. Once Bob played football for the ship's team against another ship, but after the game he was not allowed to eat with the other players and had to wait outside.

In 1964 Bob visited the southern states of America during the Civil Rights movement and in New Orleans again experienced racism. He went into a bar and was asked for his ID card. Bob showed it and asked the barman if he really thought he was under age. The barman said, 'No, that's got nothing to do with it. It's your colour.' Bob asked why and was told: 'If you were American

we would have chucked you out, but as you're a British visitor, we don't want to cause any problems.'

In 1965 Bob went to Jamaica and lived in Kingston for a while where he found the colour of his skin did not matter. He married a Jamaican woman, whom he met in England where she was studying nursing, and he took out Jamaican nationality.

Bob has been involved in the trade union movement since he was fifteen. He was a convener in the National Union of Seamen and a shop steward on the Isle of Wight ferries. In 1974-1976 he went back to Jamaica and became the National Research Officer for the National Workers' Union of Jamaica, working with the prime minister Michael Manley.

In 1976 he was back in England and working as Research and Education Officer for the Transport and General Workers Union in the south of England. In 1989 he became National Secretary for Equalities at the TGWU and has responsibilities for race, youth and sexuality issues throughout the whole of the UK and Ireland. As such he has worked in Denmark, Italy, Germany, France, Spain and Austria, lecturing and advising on race equality issues.

He is currently the Vice Chair of the European Monitoring Centre on Racism, in Vienna. Bob also sits on the English Sports Council's Race Advisory Committee and is involved in the 'Kick Racism out of Football' campaign. He was a football referee for fourteen years and has worked closely with Garth Crooks.

Bob sees the advantages of belonging to more than one culture and tradition. He traces his English background from his mother and stepfather back to the twelfth century, has recently investigated his father's roots in Arizona and Arkansas, and also sees himself as Jamaican.

He has two daughters. One has already graduated in Chinese and French and speaks six languages; the other is at Loughborough University studying Psychology and is in the Great Britain sprint team.

RAY SEFIA

Ray Sefia is the director of the Centre for Employment and Enterprise Development in Bristol and has worked as a local councillor in the city.

He was born in 1955 in Birmingham to a Nigerian father and an English mother. His mother, who came from Birmingham, worked as a tax inspector and his father, who was training as a journalist, was working as a manager of a restaurant when they both met. They had six children and Ray was the oldest.

When he was six the family moved to Nigeria and Ray was sent to live in Ovwian, his native Urhobo village, to learn to behave and receive typical African discipline. This sometimes involved getting up at 4am to go and tap rubber, pour the latex into a bucket, smoke it and then sell it to the rubber company. He also had the job of fetching water and sweeping the compound with a bamboo brush. First thing in the morning he had to wash his mouth out and chew a chewing-stick before greeting the elders of the village. He was brought up by the community, swam in the river, hunted in the forest and went fishing with his uncle during the night.

After finishing primary school Ray received a scholarship to go to a boarding school called Government College Ughelli, where he took his Secondary School Certificate. At one time he was expelled for organising a protest against the injustice inflicted on another student. The Minister of Education had to intervene and he was allowed back to sit his exams. After school he worked for a civil engineering company, first as a pay-roll clerk and then as an accountant.

At the age of 21 he returned to England, to stay with his mother who had remarried, to an Irishman, and was living in

Skelmersdale, Lancashire. There he had a culture shock, having to learn how to buy a round of drinks in a pub, how to sign on for the dole and how to pay his mother for the housekeeping.

He soon started buying and exporting clothes to Nigeria and opened a boutique in Liverpool. At the same time he went to Stockport College of Technology to take a course in Business Studies and then gained a Postgraduate Diploma in Personnel Management from Manchester Polytechnic. He also worked for SPIN (Services for People In Need) helping to set up community groups and also for the Toxteth Activities Group, during which time he undertook an MBA (Masters in Business Administration) programme with Liverpool Business School.

Ray moved to Bristol in 1992 as director of the Positive Action Consortium where he became chair of the Avon Race Equality Forum and the South West African-Caribbean Council. In 1995 he was elected as the only black councillor in Bristol, out of a total of 68.

He has set out to expose the connection between Bristol and the slave-trade, which had long been hidden, as there was no trace of it in the city's museums, and he acted as a consultant for the BBC television programme *Unequal Opportunities*. There is now a Bristol Slave-Trade Action Group and a guided tour of the parts of the city related to the slave-trade. This has caused some controversy, but in response Ray quotes Kwame Nkrumah, the first leader of independent Ghana: 'The secret of life is to have no fear.'

He sings a song expressing ancient African philosophy:

> *You do good*
> *You do for yourself*
> *You do bad*
> *You do for yourself*
> *Good is never lost*
> *Bad is never lost*
> *Anything you do*
> *It will follow you for ever. Ah! Ah!*

In 1995 Ray brought together a number of organisations in the city to form the Centre for Employment and Enterprise Development (CEED). Its mission is to improve the economic well-being of those who are disadvantaged in the community, especially those from black and other minority groups. It provides training, employment and enterprise development support, with an 80% success rate of people gaining employment. Facilities include a multimedia centre and conference hall, and from being 100% grant-aided it is now only about 4% dependent on grants.

According to Ray, black unemployment is one of the key indicators of race relations today. There has been some improvement recently because of the economic boom, but this could be reversed if there was a recession. He thinks there should be a lot more black people in politics, education and business, and those who are involved should be visible and act as role models for young people.

Ray is married to an Ibo woman from Nigeria and has twin sons aged four. His chief hobby is being an African music DJ for parties and on the radio. He has a collection of over 1,000 CDs. He also enjoys playing table tennis.

Both sides of his cultural heritage are valuable, particularly the African emphasis on community and looking after one another. Ray says: 'No culture is superior to another, just different. The beauty of diversity is to recognise the differences. A lot of mixed-race kids don't seem to know where they're coming from, don't seem to know their history, get confused and maybe hold it against their parents.' He believes in the importance of mixed-race children knowing about the culture and language of both parents in order to be sure of their self-concept.

CATHY TYSON

Cathy Tyson is the star of the film *Mona Lisa* and she is famous as a television and theatre actress.

She was born in Kingston Upon Thames, Surrey, but then moved to Liverpool where she spent the first eighteen years of her life. Her mother, who was part-Irish and worked as a senior social worker, brought her up in a working-class area of the city.

Cathy's father was a barrister from Trinidad, in the West Indies, who, although he was absent, helped her survive the racism she experienced. As she says: 'Whenever anybody called me nigger, I would say, "My father's a barrister." It's the only thing that I had to cling on to. I used that to bolster me up. I've got my father to thank for that. Even though he wasn't there in the flesh, he was there in spirit.'

At her Catholic secondary school, St. Winifred's, Cathy had three hours of drama every Friday morning, which included improvisation, and she also played a sergeant in the school play. She is very thankful for this introduction to acting. After leaving school she went to college for a while to study drama. Both her parents supported her in this choice of career.

In her early teens she attended the Rathbone Theatre Workshop on a Government training scheme for a year and then joined the Everyman Youth Theatre. Her first professional engagement was at the Everyman Theatre in Liverpool where she appeared in *The Blitz Show* followed by Miranda in *The Tempest*.

Her favourite parts are Carol in the television series *Band of Gold* and two Shakespearian roles: Kate in *The Taming of the Shrew* and Portia in *The Merchant of Venice*. Other leading theatre roles which she has played include Ophelia in *Hamlet*, Rita in *Educating Rita*, Eliza Doolittle in *Pygmalion* and Regan in *King Lear*.

Cathy has acted in several films, including *Business As Usual* and *The Serpent and the Rainbow*. She has also performed in numerous television programmes, for example *Scully*, *The Lenny Henry Show*, *Rules of Engagement*, *Angels*.

She says that she uses the same technique for any role and the qualities needed to be an actress are honesty, commitment and ability: 'Acting is tough but fulfilling. When out of work, you particularly need discipline, as you are in charge of your own time. You need to keep the flame burning and perfect your craft.' She prefers acting in the theatre in front of a live audience: 'It's nerve-racking and tense, but you feel the emotion of the audience - a thousand hearts in the National Theatre.'

When she is not working, Cathy enjoys dancing and travelling and she goes to the gym to keep fit. She also has a ten-year-old son who has seen her acting on the stage. All children, she thinks, should be encouraged to go to the theatre.

Cathy sees the value of role models, particularly strong and confident women: 'To see people who believe in themselves is very attractive. It gives people faith in them. The word role model wasn't used when I was a child, so consequently I didn't look around for them and didn't realise their importance. Ironically it's at this stage in my life that I'm starting to want them and indeed have found them.'

A BBC Radio Merseyside journalist once asked Cathy if she was mixed-race. When she said 'Yes', he asked her which part of her was mixed-race, to which she quickly replied: 'The right-hand side!'

As she says: 'The more we mix, the better we learn from each other. I'm not black or white, but what we should do with mixed race is celebrate the differences. There's a different person come into the world. Let's celebrate new things.'

MAUD SULTER

Maud Sulter is a poet and photographer.

She was born on the 19 September 1960 in Glasgow. Her mother is Scottish, of Huguenot ancestry (French protestant refugees), and her father, who worked as an eye surgeon in the Ivory Coast, was a Fante from Ghana.

Her grandfather was also an important person in her life, as he looked after her when her mother went out to work. He was interested in writing, music and photography and wrote his autobiography for her, which she found very useful when growing up. He was very precious to her and encouraged her to write poetry. On her fourth birthday he wrote a poem for her, which she found very moving.

At first Maud did very well at school, but during adolescence she got bored with it and now thinks that 'school goes on far too long'. When she left school, she worked in a shop in Glasgow and enjoyed it more than any other job she has done: 'I liked selling things to people and when the day was over you left your work behind.'

In 1977, Maud came to London and took a course at the London College of Fashion. She then studied art history and design, being particularly interested in women artists. Subsequently she did an MA in Photographic Studies at the University of Derby. Now she is completing a PhD on the impact of digital imaging on nineteenth-century images of women of African descent.

In the early 1980s Maud worked for the feminist publisher Sheba and was a member of the National Union of Journalists. She started making photographic collages and exhibiting her work. Her first solo exhibition was called *Sphinx*, at the Pavilion Gallery in Leeds. It consisted of large black and white landscape photographs of a slave-shipping island off the west coast of Africa.

She also attended a black writing workshop in Leeds with the Guyanese poet Grace Nichols and the novelist Caryl Phillips, who was born in St Kitts in the West Indies. Soon after this, Akira Press published her first collection of poems, entitled *As A Black Woman* (1985). This was followed in 1989 by another book of poetry *Zabat: Poetics of a Family Tree.* She says that the main theme of her poems is love and relationships.

One of the poems from the first volume is entitled *If Leaving You*:

If leaving you
was as easy
as the falling
in love
with
a
total
stranger

- not total

our blackness
a bond
before speech
or encounter

I could walk
from you now
into the hustle
and bustle
of Waverley
station
and checking
my ticket
- depart.

Maud enjoys going to Africa and has visited many African countries. She considers Ghana as a second home, identifies with the country culturally and spiritually, and would be perfectly happy to settle there. She also identifies with the President, Jerry

Rawlings, as he is of Scottish and Ghanaian descent, and this has proved very useful for her as an individual. Maud thinks of herself as both Scottish and Ghanaian and would like to have dual nationality. She sees a similarity in the clan and family structures of both countries and their loyalty to tradition.

Although she has occasionally experienced the pressure to choose one culture or the other, Maud feels incredibly privileged and fortunate to have access to such powerful cultural diversity. Nevertheless her advice to the parents of children with dual heritage is: 'Let them be Black. They have so much power to gain from it and nothing to lose.' At the same time she believes it is important to try and overcome the rejection that often comes from the white side of the family. One thing that she thinks would improve race relations is 'a genuine appreciation of Black culture and a recognition of its contribution, power and strength'.

Maud's main interest is in art and putting on exhibitions. She has exhibited and lectured all round Britain, as well as in the rest of Europe, Australia, Canada, USA and South Africa. She has been interviewed several times on television and radio, and edited a book on the history of art called *Passion: Discourses on Black Women's Creativity*.

MARK SEALY

Mark Sealy is a curator of international photography exhibitions and the director of Autograph, the Association of Black Photographers.

He was born in Hackney, London in 1960. His father came from Barbados where he worked in the docks. In his early 20s he left the Caribbean, without telling his mother, responding to the offer of jobs in Britain. On arrival he worked as a turner and fitter in an engineering works. Mark's mother comes from Leeds. She left school as soon as possible to travel to London, where she worked as an orderly in a hospital, eventually becoming a nurse. Mark lived in an area with lots of black children, Jews, Poles and other European immigrants and got on well at school. He has many memories of those early years: shop-lifting, having an electric shock, eating sugar sandwiches, drawing and building models. He was fascinated by horror movies and collected horror posters. He remembers his dog Lucky being run over and he also had a silver-grey kitten called Fluffy. He was very competitive with his brother who was a year older and was often protected by his sister who was four years older, but generally they all got on well together.

The family moved to Newcastle when Mark was nine years old and he and his brother found themselves to be the only black pupils in his new school. He coped well, however, as his mother had instilled in him confidence and a sense of self-worth. She had prepared him for the racism he would encounter.

After leaving school he did a few labouring jobs to earn money and then went to a Sixth Form College. He completed his education by going to Art School at Goldsmith's in London, where he did a textile degree. He also became interested in

film, photography and journalism.

His first job was as a researcher for the Daily Mirror, working in the library and filing cuttings. He then worked for three years with a picture agency called Network Photographers. Meanwhile he was also curating shows of black artists, particularly photographers who were dealing with the representation of race.

Mark sees art, not as providing solutions, but as stimulating ideas and offering a multitude of perspectives. This ties up with his view of mixed-race people as 'complex individuals with a range of different historical backgrounds'. He does not like them being pigeon-holed and knows that there is a variety of black experiences: 'Judge people on what they do, how they act, what they say, what they leave behind.'

In 1991, Mark became director of Autograph, the Association of Black Photographers, which is funded by the Arts Council of England and the London Arts Board. The organisation was set up in 1988 after a lot of pressure by black artists. As Mark says: 'People will give you nothing unless you actually fight for it.'

In 1993 he put on an audio-visual programme in the old Roman amphitheatre at Arles, in France. He has also staged exhibitions in the USA and Brazil, as well as selling works to the Victoria & Albert Museum in London. Recently he has edited a couple of photographic books and he has lectured throughout the UK and abroad. Mark describes his work as advocacy, helping not only established practitioners, but new photographers as well, to develop their careers. He believes in high standards and being frank in his assessment of people's work.

His other interests are football (he is a Newcastle United fan), reading and popular culture, particularly jazz. He does not think he belongs to more than one culture, but feels black and British. Although he has visited his father's family, he does not see the Caribbean as home. Mark believes it is important for mixed-race people not to see themselves as unique and isolated, but to feel that they belong. His advice to parents of mixed-race children is simply: 'Just love your kids.'

OONA KING

Oona King is only the second black woman MP to be elected to the British House of Commons.

She was born in Sheffield, south Yorkshire, and has a very mixed cultural heritage. Her mother came from a working-class Jewish family in Newcastle upon Tyne. Her grandfather was Hungarian and her grandmother had Scottish and Irish parents. Oona's African-American father came from Georgia. He was involved in the Civil Rights movement and lived in political exile for 35 years.

Oona now lives in the East End of London and she is learning Bengali. As she says: 'For me, racism is not an academic point. I am "multi ethnic". I have been called yid, nigger and half-caste. I love the East End because it is Britain's answer to Manhattan's melting pot.'

When her parents divorced Oona was brought up by her mother in Camden, north London, where she went to a comprehensive school. During the holidays she visited her father in Kenya and Australia.

When she left school Oona visited Nicaragua as a field labourer and then went to York University where she gained a first class degree in Politics. She worked for five years as an assistant to Labour Members of the European Parliament in Brussels, Belgium, where she met her Italian husband, Tiberio Santomarco. After that she worked as the regional organiser of the General, Municipal and Boilermakers' Union in Surrey. She has always been an active trade unionist and has run race-awareness courses in the trade union movement.

When she was four years old Oona had the ambition to be Prime Minister, though she outgrew this idea by the age of twelve.

'It wouldn't suit me,' she says. On 1 May 1997, at the age of 29, she was elected as the Labour Member of Parliament for the constituency of Bethnal Green and Bow . Despite being elected, she says her most difficult achievement was 'becoming an aerobics teacher'. Keeping fit is important to her and she admits that gaining the aerobics qualification was harder than her degree.

Oona wants to have children but realises how difficult this is as an MP. Since entering Parliament she has exhausted herself. She catches up on sleep 'at the weekend at the expense of sorting my life out. I've never done the washing, paid the bills, bought the birthday presents I ought to or written to my dad.'

The responsibility of being one of only two black women in the House of Commons is recognised by Oona: 'Because the black community is so under-represented in Parliament, it is not a representative democracy. I am a constituency MP who represents members outside my constituency.' She is also interested in women's issues. Her message to younger black women is: 'If you are black you have to work twice as hard to get half as far. If you are a black woman you have to work four times as hard to get a quarter as far.'

Her first action in Parliament was to table a bill to ensure councils consider equal opportunities policies when they contract work out. This will help the long-term unemployed and particularly the disproportionately high numbers of young black people out of work. As Oona says: 'It is often the black community that's been hardest hit by privatisation in local government. I'm over the moon that I've got the opportunity to change the law in an area that'll help our communities.'

In her first year as an MP, Oona visited Bangla Desh to find out more about the background of many of her constituents and went on a government fact-finding mission to Uganda, Rwanda and Kenya.

LEONE ROSS

Leone Ross is a journalist and novelist, presently editor of the *Black Media Journal*, a new quarterly arts magazine.

She was born in Coventry in 1969 to a Scottish father and a Jamaican mother. Both her parents were art students who eventually settled in London, but separated soon afterwards. In 1975 Leone's mother decided to return to the Caribbean, determined that her six-year-old daughter should be raised in a country where the majority of the population was black.

As her mother was a feminist and a member of the communist Workers Party of Jamaica, Leone became involved in politics as early as ten years old, giving speeches and travelling to the Soviet Union as a representative of the WPJ's youth wing. In 1981 she spent several months in post-revolutionary Grenada while her mother worked for the government as a journalist.

At primary school in Jamaica Leone was seen as 'the white girl' and was teased by other girls. The boys came to her rescue, as she recalls: 'I remember a glorious fight that took place in the middle of the yard when the boys just completely lost it and started beating up the girls who were beating me up.' She wanted to be seen as Jamaican and made sure she could speak patois.

Leone enjoyed school and did particularly well in English Literature. She was a member of the student council, editor of the school magazine and president of the drama society. At one time she wanted to be an actress and was involved in amateur theatre activities across the island.

After school she went to the University of the West Indies where she received a first class honours degree in Literature and Social Science. Then she came back to England where she completed a masters degree in International Journalism at City University, London.

When Leone returned to England, at the age of twenty, she learned more about racism and aligned herself with the black community: 'I found that even though the black community embraced me, there was and still is a lot of pain associated with acknowledging my racial identity as a whole. I am a black woman: a 'mixed-race' black woman. I am no better, not superior, just different. I have a white father, which implies a different emotional and psychological space. I am a black woman, which implies the same political and social space.'

Leone says that 'being part of two cultures is a very difficult place to be in'. She has never felt white, only mixed-race or black. She sees herself as Jamaican culturally. When her grandparents took her to Scotland to see her roots she felt very little emotional connection with this past. It made her sad.

Nevertheless she does thank her father personally for his belief in her ability to tell stories: 'He is a very creative man. He was always my biggest fan. He always knew that I could do it. I am my father's daughter: introspective, creative, worried, intense. In the same way I am my mother's daughter: sociable, articulate, political.'

Leone's interest in journalism started from an early age, when she used to help her mother, transcribing her interview tapes. She was able to earn money from this work at the age of fifteen, when she also started writing articles and reviews. By eighteen she was doing work for Jamaican dailies and some of her poems were published in an anthology. She also worked in the Caribbean for the Inter Press news agency and the BBC.

In England Leone continued her journalistic career, specialising in race, gender and sexuality politics, as well as entertainment reporting. She has worked primarily for the black press, as desk editor and writer at *The Voice* and *Pride*, researcher for London Weekend Television, women's editor at the *New Nation* and deputy editor at the feminist magazine *Sybil*.

But her ambition was always to write novels, her favourite writers being Toni Morrison, Gabriel Garcia Marquez, Isabel Allende and Stephen King. Her first novel *All the Blood is Red*, which took six months to write, came out in 1996 and is the story of 'four women with laughter in their hearts, power in their spirits

and beauty in their souls, reaching for dreams the whole world seems to want to destroy'. Her second novel *Orange Laughter*, about a black man living under the streets of New York who is gradually going mad, was published in 1999.

Leone is a huge Prince fan, reads tarot cards and does amateur horoscopes, enjoys yoga, swimming and doing embroidery, likes film, theatre and television chat-shows. She describes herself as a feminist humanist.

TUNDE JEGEDE

Tunde Jegede is a musician and composer, celebrated for his playing of the kora or African harp-lute, as well as being an accomplished cellist.

He was born in London in 1972 to a Nigerian father and an English mother, with Irish connections, who was born near Macclesfield in Cheshire. His mother grew up in Cornwall where her father was a church organist and choirmaster. He encouraged Tunde and gave him his love of western classical music.

Both of Tunde's parents are artists and from an early age he played the drum in his father's poetry and percussion group. At the age of five he performed live on Alex Pascal's radio show *Black Londoners*. His father worked as an artist at the Keskidee Centre, Britain's first Black Arts Centre, where Tunde met many famous black cultural figures such as Bob Marley and Linton Kwesi Johnson.

When Tunde was nine he was awarded a scholarship to the Purcell School of Music where he studied the cello with Joan Dickson and later went to the Guildhall School of Music and Drama. He read Joseph Conrad's novel *Heart of Darkness* for A level English Literature and successfully challenged his teacher about the author's racism.

He also studied the music of the ancient griot (poet and oral historian) tradition of Mali and in 1982 went to The Gambia to learn to play the kora. The family of his present teacher is one of four in a guild of hereditary poet-musicians and Tunde is one of only a few from outside these families to be allowed to study this tradition.

He has performed his own music on the harp-lute as a soloist in many concerts, as well as on the radio and television. In 1988

his sister, five-year-old Maya Jobarteh, gave her first public performance with Tunde at the Shaw Theatre in London. He has contributed to the albums of many artists such as Caron Wheeler and Trilok Gurtu, as well as releasing his own two recordings *Lamentation* and *Malian Royal Court Music*.

At the age of fifteen Tunde discovered African-American music and was particularly influenced by the music of John Coltrane and Miles Davis. He began to explore the links between jazz and traditional African music. Bob Marley's reggae music was his first love and his favourite orchestral composers are Bach, Shostakovich and Stravinsky.

Recently Tunde has been researching the composer and violinist, Joseph Emidy (1775-1835), an ex-slave who eventually settled in Cornwall. This is part of a project called *Hidden Routes* which brings together social history and the arts.

As Tunde says: 'I have know for a long time that there were people of African descent making classical music. What interests me is what life was like for him back then and how his journey influenced his music. I think that his works might well demonstrate a direct link to the classical instruments like the harp-lute that came out of pre-colonial Africa.' The only known picture of Emidy is in the National Portrait Gallery, but Tunde has already tracked down his great great granddaughter in Chicago and found works by his son and grandson.

He has also been involved, as a project leader, in an education programme called *Miracles*, which involved ten boroughs in west London, culminating in a Royal Gala performance in the Albert Hall, in which many of the young people from the project participated. Tunde has written and lectured on music and apart from this central concern his main hobby is football.

In his playing and composing Tunde has managed to reflect the cultures of both his parents, the musical traditions of Africa, America and Europe. He sees the spiritual dimension to music as crucial: 'Experience and inspiration are the main elements in composing and performing music.' He has given many recitals of his music around the world, including Belgium, Holland, Germany, Ireland, Morocco and the USA.

PART TWO

Historical Biographies

ROBERT WEDDERBURN

Robert Wedderburn was a revolutionary who campaigned for the abolition of slavery and for the common ownership of the land.

He was born in Jamaica in 1762. His father, James Wedderburn, was a Scotsman who owned large sugar estates on the island, which was why Robert was born free. His mother was a slave called Rosanna and his grandmother, Amy, although also a slave, earned a living selling goods in Kingston. When he was eleven years old, Robert saw his grandmother being beaten by her master. He also saw his mother flogged.

At 16, Robert joined the navy and in 1778 landed in England. He saw action against the French aboard a British man o'war and complained about the savage floggings inflicted on sailors, which reminded him of how the slaves were treated in Jamaica. After some years at sea he settled in London where he became a skilled tailor. He lived in St Giles in an area called the 'rookeries' where fellow 'blackbirds' scraped a living as musicians, actors, street entertainers, prize fighters and casual labourers.

Around 1786 Wedderburn was converted to Methodism after hearing a Wesleyan preacher addressing a crowd in Seven Dials. Later, in 1813, he became a revolutionary and follower of Thomas Spence who argued that private land should become public property.

In 1817 Wedderburn produced several editions of a magazine called *The Axe Laid to the Root*. In the first edition he writes: 'Wedderburn demands, in the name of God, in the name of natural justice, and in the name of humanity, that all slaves be set free. I am a West Indian, a lover of liberty, and would dishonour human nature if I did not show myself a friend to the liberty of others.' In the second edition he addresses the slaves of Jamaica: 'It is necessary for you to know how you may govern yourselves without a king, without lords, dukes, earls, or the like.'

Wedderburn was licensed as a minister and was known as the 'Black Prince', but his preaching, in Hopkins Street Chapel, was mainly concerned with getting rid of slavery and establishing equality in society. The atmosphere in the

chapel was more like a debating society, with singing, acting, clowning and laughter, as well as serious discussions. Spies were sent by the government to his chapel, which was actually a hayloft.

The government feared his powers of public speaking and the Home Secretary called him a 'notorious firebrand'. In 1820, as a result of his fiery speeches, Wedderburn was arrested and sentenced to two years in Dorchester Jail. This was 150 miles from London, too far for his wife to afford to visit him. He was, however, visited by another famous abolitionist, William Wilberforce, who gave him two books. If he had not been in jail, he may well have been hanged for being involved with the Cato Street conspirators.

After being released from jail, Wedderburn continued his political agitation. In 1824 he published his autobiography, entitled *The Horrors of Slavery*, in which he writes: 'I should have gone back to Jamaica, had I not been fearful of the planters; for such is their hatred of any one having black blood in his veins, and who dares to think and act as a free man, that they would most certainly have trumped up some charge against me, and hung me.'

He lived long enough to see the abolition of West Indian slavery in 1834, but died in poverty the following year, aged seventy-two. As he wrote in his autobiography: 'I thank my God, that through a long life of hardship and adversity I have ever been free both in mind and body: and have always raised my voice in behalf of my enslaved countrymen.'

DIDO LINDSAY

In the eighteenth century Dido Lindsay supervised the dairy and poultry yard of Lord Mansfield's estate in Kenwood, north London, and acted as his secretary.

Mansfield was Chief Justice from 1756 to 1788 and in the Somerset case of 1772 made the most famous judgement regarding slavery. He ruled that in England a master had no power to compel a slave on board a ship or to send him back to the plantations.

Dido's father was Sir John Lindsay, a captain of the Royal Navy, and her mother was taken prisoner by Lindsay from a Spanish ship, though it is not clear whether she was stolen or rescued. Lindsay provided generously for Dido in his will in 1788.

She spent the first thirty years of her life in Kenwood, Hampstead, the home of her great-uncle William Murray, who in 1776 became the first Earl of Mansfield. There she had the responsibility of looking after the cows and chickens. Lord Mansfield and his wife had no children and enjoyed raising Dido and her cousin Lady Elizabeth Murray whose mother had died when she was a child. Dido was a playmate for Elizabeth and a portrait of the two as young women shows them walking happily arm-in-arm at Kenwood. Dido was then about fifteen and her appearance ten years later, in a portrait by Zoffany, proves her to have developed into a beautiful young woman.

She worked as Lord Mansfield's secretary and he paid her a quarterly allowance. At her father's death she inherited one thousand pounds and Lindsay's obituary in the *London Chronicle* reported that her 'amiable disposition and accomplishments have gained her the highest respect'. She received a further £500 plus £100 a year for life from her great-uncle in his

Dido and Lady Elizabeth Finch Hatton by Johann Zoffany

will. He also made certain to confirm that she was free, in order to protect her future.

Little is known about Dido after her father died, though in 1794 her name changed to Dido Elizabeth Davinier and she left Kenwood. It is thought that she probably married a clergyman.

GEORGE BRIDGTOWER

George Polgreen Bridgtower (sometimes spelt Bridgetower) was a musical prodigy: a soloist and principal violinist in professional orchestras at the age of twelve.

His father came to Europe from Barbados in the 1770s and by 1780 was living in Austria where he was the personal servant to a prince. He had married a white woman who bore him two sons. George was the older one and was born in 1779 in Biala, Poland.

From his earliest childhood George showed extraordinary musical talent and there is a strong possibility that he was taught by Haydn. His first professional performance was at the age of nine in Paris, where he played a violin concerto. A few months later his father brought him to England where a courtier described his playing: 'The young performer played to perfection, with a clear, good tone, spirit, pathos, and good taste.'

Soon there were highly successful concerts in London, Bath and Bristol. The *Bath Journal* (7 Dec 1789) wrote of the 'astonishing abilities of this wonderful child' and of the 'exquisite performance of Master Bridgtower, whose taste and execution on the violin is equal, perhaps superior, to the best professor of the present or any former day'.

In 1791, George came under the protection of the Prince of Wales who appointed tutors for him and engaged famous musicians to teach him musical theory. By the age of 12 he was recognised by London's music-lovers as a respected member of the artistic community. Between 1789 and 1799 he performed in about fifty concerts in theatres such as Covent Garden, Drury Lane and the Haymarket.

For 14 years the young Bridgtower held the post of first violinist in the Prince of Wales's private band, which played in Carlton

George Bridgtower

House in London and in the Brighton Pavilion. In 1802 he made a concert tour of Germany and Austria and visited his mother in Dresden.

In 1803 he made friends with Beethoven who was ten years older. Beethoven described him as 'a very able virtuoso and an absolute master of his instrument'. At the first performance of the 'Kreutzer' sonata Bridgtower had the difficult task of playing one movement from the composer's almost illegible manuscript. He was brave enough to alter a brief passage, at which Beethoven jumped up and hugged him, exclaiming: 'Once more, my dear fellow!' Beethoven had originally dedicated the sonata to Bridgtower.

Samuel Wesley, who performed with Bridgwater for several years, also had a high opinion of him, ranking him 'with the very first masters of the Violin': 'It was a rich treat for a lover of the instrument to hear him perform the matchless and immortal solos of Sebastian Bach, all of which he perfectly retained in memory and executed with the utmost precision, and without a single error.'

Bridgtower's younger brother was also a musician. He made a

Master Bridgtower by Henry Edridge

living playing the cello in Dresden and came to London in 1805 to perform at a benefit concert for his brother.

George Bridgtower took the degree of Bachelor of Music at Cambridge in 1811 and the anthem he composed as an examination exercise was performed there. He also composed a set of studies for the piano. In later life he travelled abroad, particularly in Italy. He died on 29 February 1860 in Peckham, south London, in poverty and was buried in Kensal Green Cemetery.

As a child prodigy, George Bridgtower was comparable to Mozart in his playing and he became one of the most famous musicians of his time.

WILLIAM DAVIDSON

William Davidson was a revolutionary at the beginning of the nineteenth century, fighting to bring down one of the most repressive governments Britain has ever seen.

He was born in Kingston, Jamaica, in 1786. His father was the island's white attorney-general and his mother was black. He was educated in Jamaica until he was about 14 and then, against his mother's wishes, was sent to Edinburgh to complete his education.

William was apprenticed to a Liverpool lawyer, but after three years ran away to sea and was twice forced into the navy. After his discharge he studied mathematics in Aberdeen for a while and then became apprenticed to a cabinet-maker in Lichfield where he became extremely skilled at his job.

It was in that Staffordshire town that William Davidson met and fell in love with a Miss Salt. But her father objected, fired a bullet through his hat and had him arrested on a false charge. Miss Salt was sent far away and later married another man. When Davidson heard the news he tried to poison himself, but was saved by a friend who gave him a strong antidote just in time.

He eventually ended up in London where he worked as a cabinet-maker and also taught in a Wesleyan Sunday school in Walworth. He married Mrs Sarah Lane, a poor widow with four sons, and had two more sons with her. Davidson was a popular man with dark eyes and dark curly hair, who invited his neighbours to his birthday party and entertained them with wine and radical songs. His wife, children and step-children, all loved him very much, and they loved him no less when he was arrested and convicted.

It was a time of great poverty and Davidson held political

meetings in his own house, as well as attending many of the large open-air meetings of protest against the government. At one of these demonstrations in Spa Fields he helped guard the banner from capture by the police. It was a black flag with skull and crossbones and read: 'Let us die like Men and not be sold like Slaves.' All round the country people were drilling and arming themselves for an uprising.

Finally the revolutionary group which Davidson belonged to met in the Cato Street loft, off the Edgware Road, where they kept their store of home-made grenades, muskets, pistols, cartridges, swords and pikes. Because he was physically strong and a good swordsman, Davidson was posted as sentry, but they had already been betrayed by a spy and the police stormed the loft. Davidson was overpowered and led away, 'damning every Person that would not die in liberty's cause' and singing 'Scots wha hae wi' Wallace bled'.

At his trial Davidson pleaded not guilty of high treason: 'I had no intention of joining in any scheme whatever, either to put down my King, or to murder his Ministers.' He told the court: 'My house has been searched and nearly pulled down and not the slightest evidence was found to show I have been guilty of any conspiracy.' He referred to Magna Carta and defended the English tradition of resisting tyranny. Then he said: 'I have no

William Davidson resisting arrest for the Cato Street Conspiracy

objection to tender my life in the service of my country; but let me at least, for the sake of my children, save my character from the disgrace of dying a traitor. For my children only do I feel, and when I think of them I am deprived of utterance - I can say no more.'

On 1 May 1820, along with his four white comrades, Davidson died bravely on the scaffold outside Newgate jail in front of the largest crowd ever to turn out for an execution. Seven hundred men stood by to keep order and to prevent any attempt at rescue. Artillery had been drawn up and horse guards patrolled the streets.

Davidson climbed the scaffold with a firm step, bowed to the crowd and said his prayers while clasping the hand of the attending clergyman. His last words were: 'God bless you all! Good-bye.' The crowd shouted 'Murder!' and 'Hang the spies!' After he was hanged and beheaded, his widow begged King George III to be allowed to take away the mutilated remains of her husband for a decent burial, but he refused her request and the body was buried in quicklime in Newgate prison.

The famous radical journalist Richard Carlile, in prison for fighting for the freedom of the press, sent Mrs Davidson £2 and asked others to help her too. He wrote to her: 'Be assured that the heroic manner in which your husband and his companions met their fate, will in a few years, perhaps in a few months, stamp their names as patriots, and men who had nothing but their country's weal at heart. I flatter myself as your children grow up, they will find that the fate of their father will rather procure them respect and admiration than its reverse.'

MARY SEACOLE

During her life-time Mary Seacole was as famous as Florence Nightingale.

Mary was born in Kingston, Jamaica, in 1805. Her father was a Scotsman serving as an army officer. Her mother, a free black woman, ran a boarding house in Kingston where army and navy officers stayed with their families, as did many other visitors to the town.

She was also a skilled healer with knowledge based on the herbal medicines brought from Africa and developed on the plantations. Mary was taught by her mother and she learnt both Caribbean traditional medicine and also European methods. At first she practised on her doll and on cats and dogs, but later she helped her mother look after invalid officers.

Mary loved to travel. She visited England, the Bahamas, Haiti and Cuba, before marrying Edwin Horatio Seacole. Her husband died soon after the wedding and her mother shortly afterwards. In 1850 Mary helped deal with the cholera epidemic in Kingston and then set off to prospect for gold in Panama.

In October 1854 she travelled to England, determined to help the wounded in the Crimean War. When she was refused an interview, she decided to travel the 3,000 miles to the Crimea at her own expense, taking with her a large stock of medicines. On arrival she established her 'British Hotel', two miles from Balaclava and, with the help of two Jamaican cooks, provided healthy food for the soldiers.

Florence Nightingale was basically employed organising her nurses at the base hospital in Scutari. Mary Seacole, on the other hand, spent much of her time helping wounded soldiers on the battle-field. Known as 'Mother' Seacole, she also cured jaundice, diarrhoea, dysentery, severe inflammation of the chest and many other illnesses. She bandaged up the wounded on both sides of the battle, stitching up wounds and split ears, often while the guns were still firing all around her.

After the war ended in March 1856, she returned to England, but her business failed. The following year her book, *Wonderful Adventures of Mrs Seacole in Many Lands*, was published and four nights of benefit performances were held for her at the Royal Surrey Gardens, a music hall set in park grounds which could hold 10,000 people. It was packed each night, as eleven military bands turned up to play for her.

The Times of Tuesday 28 July 1857 described the event: 'Few names were more familiar to the public during the late war than that of Mrs Seacole. At the end of both the first and second parts the name of Mrs Seacole was shouted by a thousand voices. The genial old lady rose from her place and smiled benignantly on the assembled multitude, amid a tremendous and continued cheering. Never did woman seem happier, and never was hearty and kindly greeting bestowed upon a worthier object.'

Mary then decided to go to India, saying: 'Give me my needle and thread, my medicine chest, my bandages, my probe and scissors, and I'm off.' But she could not find sponsors and was not able to finance the trip herself.

She lived to an old age and continued to be recognised in the streets of London by soldiers she had helped in the

Mary Seacole's autobiography, published in 1857

Crimea. On 14 May 1881 Mary Seacole died and memory of her gradually faded.

Not until 1973 did she make news again in Britain, when a group of Jamaican women in London organised the reconsecration of her grave in the Catholic cemetery in Kensal Rise, London. On 14 May 1981 a memorial service was held to mark the centenary of her death and in 1984 her autobiography was reprinted. Mary Seacole's story has been told in several recent books and so many more people now know about her extraordinary life.

THOMAS BIRCH FREEMAN

Thomas Birch Freeman was the greatest pioneer missionary West Africa has ever known.

He was born on 6 December 1809 and baptized at Twyford, near Winchester in January 1810. His father was black, probably coming to England as a slave and then gaining his freedom, and his mother was a local white woman. His father worked as a gardener and they lived in poverty in a small cottage.

Thomas was an adventurous boy and used to frighten his mother by trying to climb a big tree in the cottage garden. In the end his father decided to cut it down to prevent an accident. When Thomas was only six years old, his father died.

Nothing more is known about his childhood, but eventually Thomas went to work as a botanist and head gardener to Sir Robert Harland, at Orwell Park, near Ipswich. He joined the Methodists, became a local preacher and spent his time visiting the sick and poor. The vicar objected and told Thomas's master, who offered him the choice of Methodism or his job. He chose Methodism.

Thomas then decided to become a missionary, as he wrote in his journal: 'I laid aside all my secular engagements and arrived at the Wesleyan Methodist Mission House, 62 Hatton Gardens, with a holy determination to spend and be spent in the important work of a Wesleyan missionary.' He was ordained in Islington Chapel, Liverpool Road, London on 10 October 1837 and the following Tuesday married Elizabeth Boot who was the housekeeper to Sir Robert and Lady Harland.

On 3 January 1838 he landed in the Gold Coast (Ghana) and on the first Sunday he took his first service at 6am in the open air. Within five months he had organised the building of a church,

levelling the floor with his own hands. A congregation of 1200 people were present at the opening of the chapel. By this time, however, Freeman had been devastated by the death of his wife through fever.

On 9 June 1840 he arrived back in England, already famous, and went on a speaking tour of all the major towns in the country to raise money for more missionaries. In November he married Lucinda Cowan, the daughter of the minister at Bedminster, Bristol, and by 1 February 1841 he was back in Africa. Tragically, less than seven months after landing, Lucy, who was pregnant, died of a fever. The death rate of missionaries was also very high.

Of 32 missionaries sent out in ten years, 15 died before they had been in the country eight months.

Freeman then went to Nigeria where he became the first Methodist missionary to that country. Although the slave-trade had been abolished in Britain in 1807, there were slavers from Spain, Portugal and Brazil still at work. Freeman was at the heart of the struggle against this trade. He visited the King of Dahomey to try and persuade him to stop selling slaves and cultivate oil-palm instead.

In 1854 he married again, this time to an African woman, and they had four children. In 1857 he resigned as a superintendent to become a civil servant, but carried on preaching. After a few years he built a house near Accra and took up market gardening. He corresponded with Kew Gardens and knew the Latin names for almost every flower and tree he came across in West Africa. He also wrote a novel called *Missionary Enterprise No Fiction*.

In 1873, at 64 years of age, he started his second period as a minister, continuing to build churches and open schools. His congregation called him Father Freeman.

At the age of 75 he took charge of the Jubilee celebrations of the Gold Coast Mission. At this time he was described as: 'a very tall, straight, stately old man, with silvery hair, perfect, courtly manners, and a splendid presence. He was never anything but dignified, and everyone treated him with profound respect. Yet he had a fund of quiet humour, and always enjoyed a good joke. He was kind and courteous to all, always accessible, and wherever he went he was loved. Children ran after him in the street, and it was quite usual to see two or three of them holding each of his hands. Kind-hearted to a degree, he was always ready to go out of his way to help people in need or to deliver the oppressed.'

Soon after the Jubilee he retired and his strength failed. He caught influenza and died, aged 81, on 12 August 1890. His last words to his son, Tom, were: 'I am like a little bird with wing ready raised for flight.'

WILLIAM WELLS BROWN

In 1853 William Wells Brown wrote the first novel in African American literature and in 1858 he wrote the first African American play to be published.

He was born around 1814 on a plantation near Lexington, Kentucky, the son of a white man who never acknowledged him and a slave woman called Elizabeth. His childhood was spent mainly in St. Louis, Missouri, where he worked as a house servant. His mother worked in the fields cultivating tobacco and hemp. William remembers hearing her being whipped by the overseer: 'Though the field was some distance from the house, I could hear every crack of the whip, and every groan and cry of my poor mother.'

William had a light complexion which often caused him difficulties, as he explains: 'The nearer a slave approaches an Anglo-Saxon in complexion, the more he is abused by both owner and fellow-slaves. The owner flogs him to keep him "in his place", and the slaves hate him on account of his being whiter than themselves. Thus the complexion of the slave becomes a crime, and he is made to curse his father for the Anglo-Saxon blood that courses through his veins.'

Later William worked as a field hand, an innkeeper's assistant, a printer's helper and an assistant in a medical office. Then he became a handyman for a slave-trader and made three trips up and down the Mississippi River between St. Louis and the New Orleans slave market.

When William finally returned to his master in 1832, he learned that he was to be put up for sale. This led to his first attempt to escape which failed partly because of his determination to take his mother with him. He suffered the usual punishment for trying to run away - beatings and hard labour in the fields.

The following year he was sold again and his new owners took him on a family trip to Cincinnati where he made his escape from slavery. He travelled by night alone in the cold from Cincinnati across Ohio to Cleveland. On his way he was helped by Mr and Mrs Wells Brown who were Quakers. William acknowledged their friendship by adding their names to his own.

Once free Brown worked for nine years as a steamboat man on Lake Erie and a conductor for the Underground Railroad which helped slaves from the south escape to freedom in the north. He lectured for the Anti-Slavery Society and was often pelted with eggs and bags of flour by those supporting slavery. In 1847 he wrote his autobiography, *Narrative of William W. Brown, a Fugitive Slave*, which went through four American editions and five British editions before 1850, earning its author international fame.

In the book he describes how a slave-owner 'tied up a woman of his, by the name of Delphia, and whipped her nearly to death; yet he was a deacon in the Baptist church, in good and regular standing. Poor Delphia! I was well acquainted with her, and called to see her while upon her sick bed; and I shall never forget her

William Wells Brown attempting to escape from slavery

appearance. She was a member of the same church with her master.'

In 1849 Brown went to Europe to attend the International Peace Congress in Paris and to encourage British support for the anti-slavery movement in the United States. He stayed in England for over five years, giving more than a thousand anti-slavery lectures 'in every town of any note in England, Ireland, Scotland and Wales', often to audiences of between three and four

William Wells Brown, drawn and engraved by R. Woodman

thousand. His tour of Scotland in 1851 was accompanied by Ellen and William Craft who also spoke at the meetings.

He also published his novel *Clotel* which tells the story of a mixed-race daughter of the American President, Thomas Jefferson, her beauty, idealism and disappointments in love. At the beginning of the book Brown comments on the growth of the mixed-race population: 'With the growing population of slaves in the Southern States of America, there is a fearful increase of half whites, most of whose fathers are slave-owners, and their mothers slaves. In all the cities and towns of the slave states, the real negro, or clear black, does not amount to more than one in every four of the slave population. This fact is, of itself, the best evidence of the degraded and immoral condition of the relation of master and slave in the United States of America.'

In 1854 Brown's friends bought his freedom and he returned to the United States where he continued to campaign for the abolition of slavery until the end of the Civil War. After the war he practised medicine in Boston and wrote several more books, including *The Rising Son; or, The Antecedents and Advancement of the Colored Race*, which contained biographical sketches of 110 famous black Americans.

FREDERICK DOUGLASS

Frederick Douglass was the most famous African American campaigner against slavery and his celebrated autobiography, *Narrative of the Life of Frederick Douglass, an American Slave*, became a best-seller.

He was born Frederick Augustus Washington Bailey in 1818 in Maryland, USA, the son of Harriet Bailey, a slave owned by Captain Aaron Anthony, who was assumed to be his father. As a child Frederick was separated from his mother and he only ever saw her four or five times, 'and each of those times was very short in duration, and at night. She was hired by Mr. Stewart, who lived about twelve miles from my home. She made journeys to see me in the night, travelling the whole distance on foot, after the performance of her day's work. She was a field hand, and a whipping is the penalty for not being in the field at sunrise.'

In 1825 Frederick was sold and went to live in Baltimore. He managed to learn to read and write, although it was forbidden, through the help of poor white children living in his neighbourhood. He used to give bread to 'the hungry little urchins, who, in return, would give me that more valuable bread of knowledge'.

At the age of twelve, Frederick realised he would be a slave for life, but from his reading he learnt that there was a campaign to abolish slavery: 'I often found myself regretting my own existence, and wishing myself dead; and but for the hope of being free, I have no doubt but that I should have killed myself, or done something for which I should have been killed.'

In 1833 he found himself working as a field hand and was constantly whipped by his overseer. Eventually he turned on the man and fought him for nearly two hours, after which he was not whipped again: 'The battle with Mr. Covey was the turning-point in my career as a slave. It rekindled the few expiring embers of freedom, and revived within me a sense of my own manhood. It recalled the departed self-confidence, and inspired me again with a determination to be free.'

Douglass made an attempt to escape in 1835, but was betrayed and put in prison. In 1838, however, posing as a free sailor, he successfully escaped to Philadelphia and then to New York. Later that

Frederick Douglass

year he married Anna Murray with whom he had four children.

By 1839 Frederick Douglass was an active member of a black abolitionist group and was soon hired to give anti-slavery lectures, touring several American states. People were astonished to hear him speak, as a correspondent to the *Liberator* wrote in 1844: 'Many persons in the audience seemed unable to credit the statements which he gave of himself, and could not believe that he was actually a slave. How a man, only six years out of bondage, and who had never gone to school a day in his life, could speak with such eloquence - with such precision of language and power of thought - they were utterly at a loss to devise.'

In 1845 his famous autobiography was published. Within three years 11,000 copies had been printed in the United States, the work had gone through nine English editions and had been translated into both French and Dutch. He then went on a speaking tour of England, Scotland and Ireland.

In 1846, Douglass was legally emancipated when Ellen and Anna Richardson of Newcastle, England, purchased his freedom for seven hundred dollars. He returned to the United States in 1847 to edit and publish various abolitionist newspapers and he became the most famous black man in the public life of his time.

In 1884 Douglass married a white woman, Helen Pitts. He was one of the few black people at this time to support intermarriage. He believed in the inevitable mixing of the two races, though he thought it would take a long time to be acceptable.

At the time of the Civil War he helped persuade President Abraham Lincoln to accept black soldiers into the Union army and in 1889 he was appointed US Minister to Haiti. William Wells Brown wrote that Frederick Douglass's career was 'more widely known than that of any other living colored man, except, perhaps, Alexandre Dumas'. W. E. B. Du Bois called him 'the greatest of American Negro leaders' and Paul Robeson described him as 'our greatest hero and teacher'. He died of a heart attack on 20 February 1895.

ELLEN CRAFT

Ellen Craft, born in Georgia in 1826, was one of the most famous American runaway slaves of the nineteenth century.

Her mother was a slave and her father was her mother's master. She had such a light skin that many people thought she was a member of the master's family. Ellen was not treated as badly as many other slaves, but the master's wife was so jealous that she took the 11-year-old girl away from her mother and gave Ellen to her own daughter as a wedding present.

When Ellen was older, she married another slave called William Craft who was a talented carpenter and cabinet-maker, and they spent a lot of time discussing how to escape from slavery. They knew that to succeed in Georgia they would have to travel a thousand miles across the slave states. One night William told Ellen of an idea he had. As she was often mistaken for a white person, she could disguise herself as his master, travel with William as her slave, and escape together to the North.

Ellen replied: 'I think it is almost too much for us to undertake; however, I feel that God is on our side, and with his assistance, notwithstanding all the difficulties, we shall be able to succeed. Therefore, if you will purchase the disguise, I will try to carry out the plan.'

It was not easy for a slave to buy clothes, but eventually William obtained them all, except the trousers, which Ellen made herself. She kept them hidden, locked in drawers in the house. She then obtained a pass from her mistress to be away for a few days at Christmas and William obtained a similar pass from the cabinet-maker to whom he was apprenticed. Neither of them was able to read the passes at that time, as it was forbidden for slaves to learn to read or write.

Ellen Craft disguised as a man

So, early in the morning on 21 December 1848, disguised as master and slave, they set off from Georgia on their perilous journey to Philadelphia. William had cut Ellen's hair short and she wore green-tinted glasses to hide her eyes. She limped, covered her face with a bandage and pretended to be hard of hearing. William explained to everyone that his master was very ill and was going to Philadelphia for better medical care. Realising that she would have to sign her name in hotel registers, she also bound up her right hand in a sling so that she could ask the receptionist to register her name for her.

The journey involved taking trains, steamers and coaches, as they travelled through South Carolina, North Carolina, Virginia and Maryland, becoming more and more nervous as they neared their destination. Their escape, however, was a success and on Christmas Day they reached Philadelphia and freedom. They stayed up the Delaware river for three weeks with a family of Quakers and as William wrote: 'This was the first act of great and disinterested kindness we had ever received from a white person.'

From there they moved to Boston where they lived for two years. William Wells Brown was the first person to publish an account of the Crafts' escape and he organised a tour for them to tell their story. In four months they spoke at 60 anti-slavery meetings.

William worked as a cabinet-maker and Ellen did needlework. Then in 1850 the Fugitive Slave Bill was enacted and their old masters sent agents to Boston to fetch them back into slavery. Even the President of the United States, Millard

Filmore, said they should be returned to the south.

Nevertheless they managed to escape by boat to Liverpool and from there went to stay with Quakers in Bristol. Then they moved to London where they went to school for a short time to learn to read and write and also started a family. They joined the campaign for the abolition of slavery and were befriended by Harriet Martineau, the famous feminist, and by Lady Byron.

In 1860 William wrote a book about their escape entitled *Running a Thousand Miles for Freedom* and in 1863 he distinguished himself at a meeting of the British Association by challenging the racist remarks of James Hunt, president of the Anthropological Society of London. In 1868, after slavery was abolished in the USA, Ellen and William and their five children returned to the United States, bought a plantation and opened a trade school for African Americans.

Ellen died in 1897, a freedom fighter like Sojourner Truth and Harriet Tubman. As she said: 'I had much rather starve in England, a free woman, than to be a slave for the best man that ever breathed upon the American continent.'

JOHN P. PARKER

John P. Parker, once a slave, became one of the most successful conductors on the Underground Railroad, helping hundreds of slaves to escape to freedom.

He was born in Norfolk, Virginia in 1827. His father was a white slave-owner and his mother a black slave. When he was eight years old he was chained to other slaves and forced to walk to Richmond, Virginia, where he was sold. He was then marched in chains, along with 400 other slaves, to Mobile, Alabama. On the way he was nearly drowned while fording a river.

In Alabama he was bought by a doctor who had two sons. John taught the two boys to hunt and fish and in return they taught him how to read and write. Although there was a law, which was strictly enforced, against slaves being taught to read or write or have books, the two boys continually supplied him with books from their father's library. As John recalls in his *Autobiography*: 'I read the Bible, Shakespeare, and the English poets in the hayloft at odd times when I was not driving the doctor to see his patients.'

When he was about seventeen John tried to run away to the north, but after many escapades he was eventually caught and jailed. He escaped but was found by the doctor and returned to Mobile where he was placed in an iron foundry to learn the trade of an iron moulder. He continually got into fights for opposing injustice, so at last the doctor decided to sell him.

John managed to persuade a widow called Mrs Ryder to buy him for $1,800. He arranged to repay her the money with interest and so buy his freedom. As he said: 'At this time I was 18, strong as an ox, and working like a steam engine, under high pressure.' He managed to pay off the money in exactly 18 months and, in

1845, as soon as his free papers were signed, he set off up the Mississippi for the north.

He settled in Ripley, Ohio, where he eventually became the owner of an iron foundry. He married Miranda Boulden from Cincinnati and bought a house next to his place of business on the bank of the river Ohio. On the other side of the river was the slave state of Kentucky and, along with others in the abolition movement, John spent the next fifteen years risking his life to help hundreds of slaves escape across the river to the north and on to safety in Canada.

1846 engraving of Ripley and the Ohio River

A reward of $1,000 was offered for him, dead or alive, so he regularly carried a pistol and a knife to defend himself. The Fugitive Slave Law, passed in 1850, permitted slave owners to go into the free states and recover their runaway slaves and it also made it illegal to assist runaways. Being caught helping slaves escape led to confiscation of property, a fine and a jail sentence. John also risked being shot or drowned in the Ohio river. While at night he smuggled slaves across the river, by day he worked in his foundry and machine shop. He patented a number of inventions, including a tobacco press and a clod smashing machine for farmers.

John and Miranda had six children, three daughters who all studied music and three sons who all became teachers. John Parker died in 1900, but his story was not published until 1996 and there is no known picture of him. But he now takes his place, alongside Harriet Tubman, in the hall of fame of those who risked their lives to rescue their brothers and sisters from slavery.

BOOKER T. WASHINGTON

Booker T. Washington rose from being a slave to become a school principal in Tuskegee, Alabama, and a leader of black America.

Washington was born in Franklin County, Virginia, in 'the most miserable, desolate, and discouraging surroundings'. He never knew his white father and was brought up by his mother, Jane, who worked as a cook on a plantation. They lived in a slave cabin and, along with his brother and sister, slept 'in and on a bundle of filthy rags laid upon the dirt floor'.

Washington never went to school, as he writes: 'I had no schooling whatever while I was a slave, though I remember on several occasions I went as far as the schoolhouse door with one of my young mistresses to carry her books. The picture of several dozen boys and girls in a schoolroom engaged in study made a deep impression upon me, and I had the feeling that to get into a schoolhouse and study in this way would be about the same as getting into paradise.'

When slavery was ended, after the Civil War, Washington describes how his mother felt: 'My mother, who was standing by my side, leaned over and kissed her children, while tears of joy ran down her cheeks. She explained to us what it all meant, that this was the day for which she had been so long praying, but fearing that she would never live to see.'

As a teenager Washington went to work at a salt furnace, often beginning work as early as four o'clock in the morning, and later worked in a coal mine. In his autobiography he remembers this experience: 'I many times found myself lost in the mine. To add to the horror of being lost, sometimes my light would go out, and then, if I did not happen to have a match, I would wander about in the darkness until by chance I found some one to give

me a light. The work was not only hard, but it was dangerous. There was always the danger of being blown to pieces by a premature explosion of powder, or of being crushed by falling slate.'

He was determined to get an education, however, so he went to night school. When he finally went to day school, in between work shifts, he noticed that all the other children had two names. He had always been called just Booker, so he invented the name Washington and told the teacher that he was called Booker Washington. He later discovered that his mother had named him Booker Taliaferro, which is why he became known as Booker T. Washington

Booker T. Washington

In the autumn of 1872 he undertook the long five-hundred-mile journey to Hampton, Virginia, to seek admission to the Hampton Institute, an industrial school for blacks and American Indians. There he cleaned buildings and classrooms to pay for his tuition. After graduating with honours in 1875, he taught at the Institute until 1881, when he was authorized to found a school for black teachers, called the Tuskegee Normal and Industrial Institute. He believed that black Americans should learn trades, 'in agriculture, mechanics, in commerce, in domestic service, and in the professions', to build up their economic position, and that equality would eventually follow.

Washington was a powerful speaker and also made a name for himself as an author. He wrote a history of black America and a biography of Frederick Douglass. But his greatest literary achievement was his own life story *Up From Slavery* which was translated into French, Spanish, German, Russian and several other European languages. He believed in self-reliance and racial solidarity and became known as 'the sage of Tuskegee'.

ANNA JULIA COOPER

Anna Julia Cooper had a lifelong commitment to the education of black people, particularly black women.

She was born in North Carolina, the daughter of a slave, Hannah Stanley Haywood, and her white master, George Washington Haywood. She was not encouraged at school and her announced intention of going to college 'was received with incredulity and dismay'. Nevertheless at the age of nine she received a scholarship to St. Augustine's Normal School, an institution which trained teachers for newly freed slaves, and at the age of eleven became a student teacher. There she met another teacher, George Cooper, whom she married in 1877, but he died only two years later and she never remarried.

She graduated from Oberlin College in 1884 and received her masters degree in mathematics in 1887, after which she moved to Washington, D. C., to become a Latin teacher at Washington Colored High School, later renamed M Street High School. In 1902 she became principal of this school which during its history educated many well-known African American professionals, artists and politicians.

In 1906 Cooper was asked to leave the school specifically because of her educational philosophy. The school board claimed that she pushed the students too hard and had them aspire too high for blacks. She was also attacked for including among the boarders in her house a male teacher, John Love, to whom she was known to be close. She later declined a marriage proposal from him. In 1910 a new superintendent invited her back to the school to teach Latin again.

Anna Julia Cooper was committed to race and gender equality and helped found the Colored Women's League of Washington,

D. C., in 1892. She was one of the few women invited to talk at the first Pan-African Conference in London in 1900, organised by, among others, W. E. B. Du Bois, after which she went on a tour of Europe.

Anna Julia Cooper

During these years of full-time employment, and active feminist and racial organisational work, she raised two foster children and adopted her half brother's five orphaned grandchildren. Also, amongst other articles and conference papers, she wrote a major black feminist book, *A Voice from the South*, published in 1892, advocating racial justice and equal rights for African American women.

In this book she makes fun of the sexism of certain famous literary men, for example: 'Lessing declared that "the woman who thinks is like the man who puts on rouge - ridiculous"; and Voltaire in his coarse, flippant way used to say, "Ideas are like beards - women and boys have none."' She also comments on cultural racism: 'There is an old proverb "The devil is always painted *black* - by white painters." And what is needed, perhaps, to reverse the picture of the lordly man slaying the lion, is for the lion to turn painter.'

In the 1910s Cooper studied for her PhD at Columbia University and in the summers at the Sorbonne in Paris. She wrote her dissertation on French attitudes towards slavery after the French Revolution and included a study of the successful rebellion of slaves in San Domingo (now Haiti). She was awarded her doctorate from the University of Paris in 1925 at the age of 67, making her the fourth African American woman to receive a PhD.

After retiring from M Street School in 1930 she continued to teach, serving as president of Frelinghuysen University, a night school for working people. She also taught classes in her own home because there were no funds for a proper building. All her life she was a champion of black women seeking higher education and, until her death, continued to write and speak about equal opportunities.

Anna Julia Cooper died in her sleep on 27 February 1964, at the age of 105.

JOHN RICHARD ARCHER

John Richard Archer was the first person of African descent to hold civic office in Britain; the first British-born black councillor, alderman, and mayor; and the first black person to become an election agent for a constituency Labour party.

He was born on 8 June 1863 in Liverpool. His father was a ship's steward who came from Barbados and his mother was Irish. When he was a boy he had a nervous breakdown and this caused him to give up his studies in medicine. He became a seaman and travelled round the world three times.

In his late twenties he and his wife, a black Canadian, arrived in Battersea in south London. Archer earned his living as a photographer and his work won many prizes. He was elected to the borough council in 1906 and, when he was elected mayor in 1913, he told the council: 'You have made history tonight. Battersea has done many things in the past, but the greatest thing it has done is to show that it has no racial prejudice, and that it recognises a man for the work he has done.'

Archer received letters of congratulation from leading members of the black community in the USA and he was featured in Du Bois's journal The *Crisis*, with photographs of Archer and his wife in their robes of office. He wrote to an American friend: 'Last week I attended a great function at the Guildhall when twenty-eight London mayors were present with the lord mayor. It filled my heart with joy to walk in the procession of mayors in that old historic building - the first time that one of our race has done so as mayor.'

When the African Progress Union was formed in London in 1918 he was chosen as president, and he held the post for three years. The Union's aims were 'to promote the general welfare of

Africans and Afro-Peoples', to set up a social and residential club in London, and to spread 'knowledge of the history and achievements of Africans and Afro-Peoples past and present'.

At its first meeting, a few weeks after the end of the First World War, Archer made a remarkable speech which was greeted with cheers by all those present: 'The people in this country are sadly ignorant with

John Archer, Mayor of Battersea

reference to the darker races, and our object is to show to them that we have given up the idea of becoming hewers of wood and drawers of water, that we claim our rightful place within this Empire. That if we are good enough to fight the wars of the country we are good enough to receive the benefits of the country. One of the objects of this association is to demand - not ask, demand; it will be "demand" all the time that I am your President.'

In 1919 Archer went to Paris as British delegate to the first Pan-African Congress. At the second Pan-African Congress, in London in 1921, he chaired a session on colonial freedom and called on the British government to respond to the colonial people's growing political demands.

In his local community Archer had an extraordinary record of service. At various times he served on the health, works, finance and valuation committees of the council, the committee responsible for baths and wash-houses, and those concerned with unemployment and tuberculosis care. He was a governor of Battersea Polytechnic, president of Nine Elms swimming club and a trustee of the borough charities. He was active in securing a minimum wage of 32 shillings-a-week for council workers. When he died in 1932, one newspaper reported: 'The poor had no better friend.'

ARTHUR WHARTON

Arthur Wharton was the world's first black professional footballer and held the first world record for the hundred yards.

He was born in Accra, Ghana, on 28 October 1865. His father came from Grenada, in the West Indies, and was the first African-Caribbean Methodist missionary in Africa, where he worked with Thomas Birch Freeman for 26 years. Arthur's mother had a Scottish father and an African mother.

Arthur went to school in west London and to colleges in Cannock and Darlington. The intention was that he should train to be a minister of religion or a teacher, but his outstanding athletic talent soon became apparent.

In July 1886 the tall, light-brown Arthur Wharton won the Amateur Athletics Association 100 yards title in 10 seconds, later ratified as the first world record. The following year he retained the title and in 1888 he turned professional.

Wharton also played football as a goalkeeper, first as an amateur for Darlington and Preston North End, then in 1889 as a professional for Rotherham Town. He later played for Sheffield United, Stalybridge Rovers, Ashton North End and Stockport County, where he ended his career in 1902. In February 1895 he became the first black player in division one of the Football League, playing for Sheffield United against Sunderland.

He was an exciting and colourful goalkeeper. One spectator recalls his extraordinary gymnastics: 'In a match between Rotherham and [Sheffield] Wednesday at Olive Grove I saw Wharton jump, take hold of the cross bar, catch the ball between his legs, and cause three onrushing forwards - Billy Ingham, Clinks Mumford and Micky Bennett - to fall into the net. I have never seen a similar save since and I have been watching football for over fifty years.'

He also excelled at other sports. He played professional cricket in the Yorkshire and Lancashire Leagues. In 1887 he rode a tricycle between Blackburn and Preston, setting a record of two hours.

Wharton was always proud to be black. At one athletics meeting he overheard two competitors boasting that 'we can beat a blooming nigger anytime'. Wharton offered to box them, but they declined. At another meeting he felt he had won his race, but was awarded a salad bowl as second prize. He smashed it and told the organising committee to make a new one out of the bits. Similarly in a ball throwing competition his two longest efforts beat all the other competitors, so he demanded both first and second prizes!

In 1890 he married Emma Lister, a plumber's daughter from Rotherham. During the 1890s he also earned his living as a publican in Rotherham and Sheffield.

Wharton spent the last twenty or so years of his life working as a miner in the pit villages of South Yorkshire. From 1913 he was employed at the Yorkshire Main colliery at Edlington, near Doncaster. He died in poverty on 13 December 1930, leaving few personl possessions except a bible and some photos, and was buried at Edlington cemetery.

Obituaries appeared in the national and local sporting press, concentrating mainly on his triumphs as an athlete. On 8 May 1997, after a successful campaign to raise money for a gravestone by Sheffield-based *Football Unites - Racism Divides*, a memorial ceremony was held at his previously unmarked plot.

At last Arthur Wharton had been recognised, not only as an outstanding athlete and footballer, but as someone who believed in social justice and who attacked racism both in his words and deeds.

W. E. B. DU BOIS

William Edward Burghardt Du Bois (pronounced *do boys*), the founder of black studies, was the most influential writer that black America has ever produced.

He was born in Great Barrington, Massachusetts, in 1868. His mother was black (with some Dutch ancestry) and his father was of French ancestry (with some African), his grandfather having come over from France in the 1750s. William's father, Alfred Du Bois, left the family soon after William was born, but his mother brought him up as a member of the Congregational Church and encouraged him to do well at school.

He describes his mother 'with all her soft brownness, - the brown velvet of her skin, the sorrowful black-brown of her eyes, and the tiny brown-capped waves of her midnight hair as it lay parted on her forehead': 'My mother and I were good chums. I liked her. After she was dead I loved her with a fierce sense of personal loss.'

William attended mainly white schools and he graduated with honours from the local high school in 1884. He describes his feelings at school: 'It dawned upon me with a certain suddenness that I was different from the others; or like, mayhap, in heart and life and longing, but shut out from their world by a vast veil. I had thereafter no desire to tear down that veil, to creep through; I held all beyond it in common contempt, and lived above it in a region of blue sky and great wandering shadows. That sky was bluest when I could beat my mates at examination-time, or beat them at foot-race, or even beat their stringy heads. Alas, with the years all this fine contempt began to fade; for the worlds I longed for, and all their dazzling opportunities, were theirs, not mine. But they should not keep these prizes, I said; some, all, I would wrest from them. Just how I would do it I could never decide: by reading law, by healing the sick, by telling the wonderful tales that swam in my head - some way.'

In 1885 Du Bois went to Fisk University in Nashville, Tennessee. This was his first visit to the South and his first experience of southern racism: 'I shall forgive the white South much in its final judgement day: I shall forgive its slavery, for slavery is a world-old habit; I shall forgive its fighting for a well-lost cause, and for remembering that struggle with tender tears; I shall forgive its so-called "pride of race", the passion of its hot blood, and even its dear, old, laughable strutting and posing; but one thing I shall never forgive, neither in this world nor the world to come: its wanton and continued and persistent insulting of the black womanhood which it sought and seeks to prostitute to its lust.'

After receiving his bachelor's degree in 1888, Du Bois gained a scholarship to Harvard University where he graduated with another bachelor's degree in 1890 and a master's degree the following year. Between 1892 and 1894 he studied history and sociology in Germany at the University of Berlin and in 1895 earned his doctorate in history from Harvard. His dissertation, on the African Slave-Trade, was published in 1896.

By this time Du Bois was teaching at Wilberforce University, a black institution established by the African Methodist Episcopal church in Ohio. There he married Nina Gomer, a Wilberforce student, and soon afterwards accepted an offer from the University of Pennsylvania to do research into the black people of Philadelphia.

In 1897 Du Bois went to teach economics, history and sociology at Atlanta University where he founded twentieth-century African American sociology with a series of reports on such topics as black landowners, the black church, the black family and black mortality. He became convinced that the distinctive artistic traditions, expressive culture, and communal values of African Americans had to be recognised and respected by both black and white Americans. These ideas were published in 1903 in his most famous book *The Souls of Black Folk*, which became known as 'the political Bible of the Negro race'.

One section of the book criticises Booker T. Washington's idea of education as being too narrow and concentrating mainly on industrial training. Du Bois insisted on black civil rights and equality of access to higher education.

In the following years Du Bois wrote poems, essays, novels, historical and political works, biography and autobiography. He also launched the *Crisis*, official magazine of the NAACP (National Association for the Advancement of Colored People). In a 1921 edition he wrote supporting the right of intermarriage, on the basis of equality: 'We say and as free men must say that whenever two human beings of any nation or race desire each other in marriage, the denial of their legal right to marry is not simply wrong - it is lewd.' He added that 'the mingling or races' had already brought forth 'mighty offspring in its Dumas and Pushkin and Coleridge-Taylor and Booker Washington'.

In 1944 his left-wing politics led to his forced retirement from Atlanta University and in 1948 he was dismissed by the NAACP from his position as director of special research. He then joined forces with Paul Robeson and others in the Council of African Affairs, an anti-colonialist organization. In 1958 Robeson wrote:'The stature and quality of Dr. Du Bois' life and work cannot be challenged: he is the foremost scholar and sage among us. He is the father of our freedom movement today. In wisdom of mind, integrity of character and selfless dedication to humanity our Dr. Du Bois is outstanding not only in Negro life: he is one of the truly great Americans of our century.'

In 1963, the year of his death, Du Bois renounced his American citizenship and became a citizen of Ghana, where he had moved a few years earlier. Through his life and work he had revolutionized African American self-perception and laid the foundation for the Civil Rights movement.

SAMUEL COLERIDGE-TAYLOR

At the beginning of the twentieth century Samuel Coleridge-Taylor won world fame as a composer of concert music.

He was born in Holborn, London, in 1875. His father came to Britain from Sierra Leone to study medicine, qualified as a surgeon and then went back to Africa where he was appointed coroner of The Gambia. His mother was English.

Samuel could read music by the age of four. When he was six years old, his musical gifts were discovered by a Croydon violin teacher who saw him playing marbles in the street, clutching a tiny violin in one hand and some marbles in the other. At the age of 15, he entered the Royal College of Music where he studied composition.

In 1896 he met the American poet Paul Laurence Dunbar, son of a former slave, and set some of his poems to music. By 1898 Elgar, then Britain's leading composer, was describing Coleridge-Taylor as 'far and away the cleverest fellow amongst the young men'. In this year came the triumphant first performance of his *Hiawatha's Wedding Feast* and he became established as one of Britain's outstanding young composers. He said his ambition was to 'do for negro music what Brahms has done for Hungarian folk-music.' From 1903 to his death in 1912, he was professor of composition at Trinity College of Music, London, and held various other teaching posts.

In 1904 he made the first of several visits to the USA and read *The Souls of Black Folk* by W. E. B. Du Bois in order to prepare himself. His hosts were an all-black choral society, the 160-strong Samuel Coleridge-Taylor Society of Washington, D.C., which had been formed in 1901 with the chief aim of bringing the composer to Washington to conduct a festival of his works.

They feared he may be insulted by racists, but Coleridge-Taylor replied: 'As for prejudice, I am well prepared for it. Surely that which you and many others have lived in for so many years will not quite kill me. I am a great believer in my race, and I never lose an opportunity of letting my white friends here know it. Please don't make any arrangements to wrap me in cotton-wool.' His visit was a triumph. Thousands of black people turned out to greet him and the critics praised both his music and his skill as a conductor.

Samuel Coleridge-Taylor wanted justice for all black people and was a firm supporter of the Pan-African movement. He organised the music for the Pan-African Conference held at Westminster Town Hall in July 1900 and was elected to the executive committee of the Pan-African Association.

He also showed solidarity with black people in unexpected ways. Once a shabby-looking man, shouldering a stick with a bundle tied up in a brightly coloured handkerchief, called at his house and asked the composer to hear him sing. The visitor turned out to have a fine voice, the result being an introduction to a London agent, with a subsequent concert appearance.

Coleridge-Taylor died of double pneumonia at the early age of 37. At the time of his death he was working on an operetta about the intermarriage of white and black people. He had married his white wife Jessie in 1899, despite her parents' objections to a mixed marriage, and left her with two children. Hiawatha, born in 1900, became a conductor, especially of his father's music. Avril, born in 1903, had a distinguished career in her own right as both composer and conductor.

WALTER TULL

Walter Tull played football for Tottenham Hotspur and was an officer in the First World War.

He was born in Folkestone on 28 April 1888. His father, a carpenter from Barbados, came to Folkestone in 1876 and married a local woman. By the age of nine, Walter had lost both his parents, his mother of cancer, aged 42, and his father of heart disease.

In February 1898 Walter and his brother Edward were sent to a Methodist orphanage in Bonner Road, Bethnal Green. His brother left the orphanage two years later, adopted by a Scottish family, and later owned a dental practice in Glasgow.

Meanwhile Walter played at left-back for the orphanage football team. He then served an apprenticeship as a printer with a view to joining a newspaper, but a letter to Clapton FC in October 1908 was to change all that. By the end of the year he was playing for their first team and within a few months had won winners' medals in the FA Amateur Cup, London County Amateur Cup and London Senior Cup. He played inside-left for the Clapton team and on 20 March 1909 the *Football Star* called him 'the catch of the season'.

In 1909 he signed as a professional for Tottenham Hotspur. He was paid a £10 signing on fee (the maximum allowable at the time) and wages of £4 a week. In September he played in Spurs' first game in the top division, a 3-1 defeat at Sunderland.

The following month Tull experienced spectator racism when Spurs travelled to play Bristol City. According to one observer, 'a section of the spectators made a cowardly attack upon him in language lower than Billingsgate'. The correspondent continued: 'Let me tell these Bristol hooligans that Tull is so clean in mind and method as to be a model for all white men who play football

whether they be amateur or professional. In point of ability, if not in actual achievement, Tull was the best forward on the field.'

In October 1911 Tull moved to Northampton Town where he played half-back and scored nine goals in 110 senior appearances. When the First World War broke out, he became the first Northampton player to join the 17th (1st Football) Battalion of the Middlesex Regiment and on 18 November 1915 his battalion arrived in France. At the trenches he continued to play football and took part in other athletic pursuits, such as tug-of-war.

When he came home from France in 1916 with trench fever, he had already risen to the rank of sergeant. On recovery he entered the officer cadet training school at Gailes in Scotland. While based there he made contact with his brother Edward, a former amateur with Ayr Parkhouse and Girvan Athletic, who arranged for him to play for Rangers.

On 30 May 1917 Tull was commissioned as second lieutenant and posted to Italy. At the first battle of Piave, during January 1918, he was mentioned in dispatches for his 'gallantry and coolness'. He then returned to France to fight in the second battle of the Somme which was to claim his life. Tull was killed instantaneously by a bullet through the head on 25 March 1918. He was awarded the British War and Victory medal and recommended for a Military Cross.

Like many who died during the Great War there is no grave for Walter Tull, who fell on the battlefield near Favreuil, France. There is, however, an inscription at the Faubourg-Amiens war cemetery.

Walter Tull was the first British-born black army officer and the first black officer to lead white British troops into battle.

NELLA LARSEN

Nella Larsen was a famous novelist of the Harlem Renaissance, the flowering of black literature in 1920s New York.

She was born Nellie Walker on 13 April 1891 in Chicago. Her mother was Danish and her West Indian father, who was a cook by occupation, came from the Virgin Islands. When she was two years old her father died and her mother married again, this time to a Danish man called Peter Larson. Nella was to change her name several times during her life, but eventually settled for Nella Larsen.

Nella was a lonely child who did not go to primary school till she was nine. In 1907 her step-father sent her to Nashville to complete high school in the Normal School Department of Fisk University, where she also began her training as a teacher. Here all the students were black, as education was segregated by law. Fisk was where W. E. B. Du Bois graduated and Booker T. Washington's son also enrolled in 1907.

Although women had equal opportunities with men, Nella was frustrated by the strict regime at Fisk. There were rules forbidding swearing, gambling, playing cards, drinking, smoking and dancing. The uniform was white blouse, navy blue jacket and skirt, and plain hat. These restrictions may explain Nella's later passion for beautiful clothes, rich fabrics and silk stockings. Among other subjects, she studied Latin, Maths, Geography and English, but never completed her teacher training.

In 1912 she went to New York and entered a training school for nurses at Lincoln Hospital, where she was consistently at the top of her class. This was one of the best nursing schools for African American women, but as Nella noted: 'All the doctors and executives in this institute were white. All the nurses were Negroes.'

After she graduated, Nella spent a year at Tuskegee Institute in Alabama as head nurse of the hospital, training student nurses. She was there when the Institute's founder, Booker T. Washington, died. The atmosphere at Tuskegee, however, was too oppressive for Nella and she returned to New York to work as assistant superintendent of nurses at Lincoln and then as district nurse in the New York Department of Health.

In 1919 she married the brilliant black research physicist, Dr Elmer Imes, and the following year saw her first publication, *Three Scandinavian Games*, in a children's magazine. In 1922 she started work as a children's librarian in Harlem and a year later achieved her certificate from the Library School. In 1926 she published two short stories in a woman's magazine and started on her first novel, though she was worried about its quality: 'The thing might turn out to be utter rot. When I first started, I honestly thought it was really good: now, something more than halfway, I'm afraid it's frightfully bad.'

The novel, entitled *Quicksand*, eventually came out in 1928. It was semi-autobiographical, about a mixed-race woman called Helga Crane who had an unhappy childhood. It had good reviews and received the Harmon Foundation Bronze Award for Distinguished Achievement among Negroes in Literature. W. E. B. Du Bois called it 'fine, thoughtful and courageous'. The next year saw the publication of her second novel, *Passing*, about two light-skinned black women from Chicago who had been childhood friends, one of whom marries a white man and passes as white.

Nella Larsen became an immediate celebrity and in 1930 was awarded a Guggenheim fellowship to travel to Spain and France to write another novel. When visiting Portugal she was fascinated by the racial appearance of the people: 'The Moors have certainly left their seed here. About 50 per cent of the population are as dark or darker than I am. And a large majority have distinctly Negroid features.'

Although starting a number of novels, however, Nella had no more published. She was divorced in 1933 and worked again part-time as a nurse, gradually cutting herself off from her former literary friends. In 1944 she began work full-time, doing night duty at a hospital in New York, where she soon became a supervising head nurse and was held in high regard.

Reading was her great joy, particularly mystery stories, and she enjoyed sewing and playing bridge. Well into her fifties she dressed in stylish clothes and wore antique necklaces, diamond rings and jade earrings. Her favourite colour was green and she wore a purple cape over her nurse's uniform.

In her early seventies, while on her way to work, she was attacked by a mugger who snatched her purse and broke her arm. But she continued to work that night and did not take any time off after the incident.

In 1964 she died of heart failure while reading in bed. At her funeral her friend and colleague Alice Carper read the eulogy: 'Nella was greatly respected and loved by her co-workers and those with whom she came in contact. No task was ever too great for her to tackle. It was inspiring and encouraging the way she worked along with those in her charge.'

Nella Larsen will be remembered mainly for her two novels, as Alice Walker writes: '*Quicksand* and *Passing* are novels that I will never forget. They open up a whole world of experience and struggle that seemed to me, when I first read them years ago, absolutely absorbing, fascinating and indispensable.'

EDNA MANLEY

Edna Manley was a world renowned sculptor and the force behind the Jamaican Art Movement.

Her father was an Englishman, a pastor who lived in Jamaica, and her mother was Jamaican. They returned to England after their first two children were born. Edna was born in Hampshire on 28 February 1900, the middle child of nine children. When she was nine years old, the family moved to Cornwall.

Edna walked to school every day with her dog Mike: 'We walked nearly two miles to school or more and this dog would go up to a certain spot on the road, and I would say "home now Mike" and he would go home. And then when it got to the time that I was due to return home from school my mother would say "Get Edna" and he would come and wait for me. Oh it was magic in Cornwall.'

Soon after they moved to Cornwall, however, Edna's father died and she describes how she wanted to be alone: 'I would run away from the house at 6 o'clock in the morning and not come home until 7 o'clock at night, out on the moors, down by the sea with nothing particular to eat. My sisters were so mad because they said I did it to avoid housework. I just don't know why I did it and I had such temper tantrums. I think the slightest thing I thought was unjust whether to me or anybody else, that was part of it. And I think it was sense of frustration. I wanted to be alone, and as a child I could not stand so many in the family.'

When she was fourteen she met her future husband, Norman, who was her cousin. He had come to England to study at Oxford. It was not love at first sight, but over a period of seven years they fell in love and when she was twenty-one they finally married.

Edna wanted to be an artist and she was always drawing

animals, horses and dogs. So she went to London to study art, but she attended four different art schools before she found a good teacher: 'I found a marvellous teacher at St. Martin who understood me and I could understand his type of discipline. I stayed with him and I always felt that he really believed in me. He would come at 9 o'clock and I would be there. And I'd stay until 11 at night if I could get the chance. His name was McCrossen. He was very Scotch and he used to say, "don't work in the round, look for the planes, lassie, look for the planes." I adored him, he was a bit like the rocks of Cornwall.'

After she finished at St. Martin's she had her first baby and then left for Jamaica at the age of 22: 'When the boat parked, if I may put it that way, there was a fantastic sky, flaming, reflected in the harbour. I thought, ah you know, this is it. A friend met us with a car and we were driving up Orange Street and there was a marvellous looking young, very black, very straight young woman, about eighteen and she was striding, and this was what I had been looking for, people who really walked. She had on her head a sewing machine, and it was at a forty-five degree angle and every now and then she would move and catch her balance. And I could nearly jump out of the car I was so excited. This movement you didn't get in England at all.'

As her husband worked at establishing his career as a lawyer, Edna attempted to settle down with the baby and to sculpting. She would sit for hours in the market place in Mandeville drinking in the scenery. This shocked some people, as a lady of 'good' family did not sit on a wall in the market place, especially if she was wearing an orange jumper. It was from this experience that she made her first carving 'The Beadseller', which, like may of her other works, is now in the National Gallery of Jamaica. A year later her second son Michael was born.

As there were no art exhibitions in Jamaica, Edna returned with her baby to England in 1923, where she exhibited in London with the Society of Women Artists. She soon realised, however, that England was not for her and she returned to Jamaica, where she had her own exhibition in 1931.

She decided not to exhibit again abroad, but join with other writers, poets and painters who were struggling to create an art movement that was truly Jamaican: 'We had some good poets - and they were writing about snow and daffodils and things they'd never seen and so we would have these terrific quarrels and tear up each other's works. It must be rooted in Jamaica, or at least the Caribbean, the climate of it, the fauna, the mountains.' This was how the Jamaican Art Movement was founded and Edna started a literary and political publication, called *Focus*, which became a forum for many young writers.

Her greatest personal encouragement came with the purchase of her sculpture 'Negro Aroused' in 1937. The piece was symbolic of the wave of nationalism that was spreading across the country. It was bought by public subscription for £100: 'It was tremendously important to me and I was touched to tears over it. If I had sold it in England it wouldn't have had the same effect but my people wanted it, my people had subscribed. This was what mattered.'

Norman, who always supported her in her work, became prime minister in 1955, which led to her giving up sculpting for seven years. She missed it, but these years were of great value to her: 'I travelled every nook and cranny of Jamaica and saw things and absorbed them: I learned a lot.'

Both her son Michael Manley, who later also became prime minister, and her husband chose politics. Edna chose art, but her art was also political. Carving as a Jamaican for Jamaica was a political act and the move to discover Jamaica and the beauty of black people was political. She insisted that Jamaican artists reflect Jamaican culture.

Her husband died in 1969: 'After Norman died, the thing that saved me was my art.' In 1975 she decided to give up sculpting, as it was too tiring for her, and took up painting. She was a striking woman with a deep clear voice and she always dressed with flair. She maintained her own identity and did not live in the shadow of her famous husband.

Edna Manley died on 10 February 1987, a few weeks short of her 87th birthday. She was passionately Jamaican. When asked, 'What do you think has been your most significant contribution to Jamaica?', her reply was: 'Loving it.'

BOB MARLEY

Bob Marley is the most famous reggae singer in the world.

He was born in the parish of St. Ann, Jamaica, on 6 February 1945, weighing six and a half pounds. St. Ann's is known as the garden parish and has a reputation of being one of the most beautiful country areas in Jamaica.

Bob's mother's name was Cedella. She had fallen in love and married a white Jamaican army officer whose name was Norval Marley. In those days mixed marriages were not common, especially in country areas, and often Cedella would be teased. Both Cedella and her husband experienced some difficulties with those who were against the relationship. However, despite these difficulties, Bob was raised as a loved and cherished little boy.

Growing up, Bob spent a lot of time with his mother and her family and he was introduced to the world of music from a very early age. His grandfather, Omeriah Malcolm, would come home after a day working in the fields and play either his violin or accordion. Bob used to love listening to his grandfather play music. His uncles were also semi-professional musicians who played instruments such as the violin, guitar and banjo.

Coming from a musical background, Bob soon gained a reputation in his local community for having a wonderful singing voice. He got to know the mento songs, which were similar to calypso songs, and he is remembered for singing one particular calypso:

> *Please mister woncha touch my tomato*
> *Touch me yam me pumpkin potato*
> *All you do is feel up, feel up*
> *Ain't you tired of squeeze up squeeze up*

Whenever that song is heard by those who knew Bob, it reminds them of him as a boy.

As Bob got older his unstoppable passion for music became more noticeable - both singing, writing songs and playing his guitar. When he told his mother that his ambition was to play music she was concerned, but eventually she supported him, recognising his determination to succeed from a very early age.

When Bob wasn't practising, which he did at every opportunity, he loved to play football. Those who knew him remember him as a young man playing on the streets of Hope Road in Kingston where he eventually went to live.

Bob was also known for his love of children. It has been said that he was quite a shy person and only came close to being himself when he was in the company of children. In the song *Lively Up Yourself* he sings: 'Never let the children cry or you'll have to tell Jah Jah why.'

By his late teens Bob had committed himself fully to his music. He had also committed himself to the teachings of the Rastafarian religion. Some say it was Bob Marley's music and his beliefs that united so many audiences, especially as he promoted the need for unity. One thing was certain: Bob would take reggae music to a new audience,

In 1973, after years of hard work, Bob Marley and the I Threes, or the Wailers as they soon became known, were beginning to get famous. The band members included Judy Mowatt, Marcia Griffiths and Rita Marley. One of the shows that led to this early fame was played at the Greyhound on the Fulham Road in London. It was then a six-piece band which also included Peter Tosh who later became a famous reggae musician in his own right. Although the band had fame, they still however did not have any money.

It was in 1976 that Bob Marley and the Wailers finally made it. They were asked to do concerts and requests for albums were ordered in advance. As Bob became more successful he released more and more albums. He used his music and his success to help forward the causes in which he believed. One example of this is the album *Zimbabwe* which took Africa by storm. The lyrics included the words: 'Zimbabwe must be free'. When Zimbabwe won its independence Bob was invited to perform at the freedom celebrations.

Songs such as *No Woman No Cry* and *I Shot the Sheriff* received world-wide acclaim, but in 1980 Bob was diagnosed as having cancer. Although he was very ill, he insisted on playing his last performance at a theatre in Pittsburgh. After that he spent his time fighting the cancer, but unfortunately the battle was lost and he died on 11 May 1981. His mother Cedella and his wife Rita were beside him when he died.

His songs live on, however, and Bob Marley's life and music continue to inspire people all round the world.

BIBLIOGRAPHY

Yasmin Alibhai-Brown & Anne Montague: *The Colour of Love: Mixed Relationships* (Virago, London 1992)

William L. Andrews et al (ed.): *The Oxford Companion to African American Literature* (Oxford University Press, Oxford 1997)

Shirley Bassey: *My Life on Record and in Concert* (Bloomsbury, London 1998)

David Boxer: *Edna Manley Sculptor* (The National Gallery of Jamaica & The Edna Manley Foundation 1990)

Allen Birtwhistle: *Thomas Birch Freeman* (Cargate Press, London 1950)

William Wells Brown: *The President's Daughter* (The X Press, London 1995)

Muriel Burgess: *Shirley* (Century, London 1998)

Pushpinder Chowdhry: *Women of Substance: Profiles of Asian Women in the UK* (Hansib, London 1997)

Stephen Davis: *Bob Marley, Conquering Lion of Reggae* (Plexus, London 1983)

Thadious M. Davis: *Nella Larsen: Novelist of the Harlem Renaissance* (Louisiana State University Press 1994)

Frederick Douglass: *Narrative of the Life of Frederick Douglass, an American Slave* (Penguin, London 1982)

W. E. B. Du Bois: *The Souls of Black Folk* (Bedford Books, Boston MA, 1997)

Dorothy Ehrhart-Morrison: *No Mountain High Enough: Secrets of Successful African American Women* (Conari Press, Berkeley CA 1997)

Bernardine Evaristo: *Island of Abraham* (Peepal Tree, Leeds 1994)

Bernardine Evaristo: *Lara* (Angela Royal Publishing, Tunbridge Wells 1997)

William Edward Farrison: *William Wells Brown: Author and Reformer* (University of Chicago Press 1969)

Peter Fryer: *Staying Power: The History of Black People in Britain* (Pluto Press, London 1984)

Lise Funderburg: *Black, White, Other: Biracial Americans Talk About Race and Identity* (William Morrow, New York 1994)

Henry Louis Gates, Jr.: *Colored People* (Vintage Books, New York 1995)

Henry Louis Gates, Jr. & Nellie Y. McKay (ed.): *The Norton Anthology of African American Literature* (W. W. Norton, New York 1997)
Gretchen Gerzina: *Black England* (Jon Murray, London 1995)
Anne Giwa-Amu: *Sade* (Ace Books, London 1996)
Nesha Z. Haniff: *Blaze a Fire: Significant Contributions of Caribbean Women* (Sister Vision, Toronto 1988)
Jacquleine Harriott: *Black Women in Britain* (Batsford, London 1992)
Lisa Jones: *Bulletproof Diva: Tales of Race, Sex, and Hair* (Penguin, London 1995)
Sandra Kitt: *Significant Others* (Onyx, Penguin, London 1996)
Cleo Laine: *Cleo* (Simon & Schuster, London 1994)
Nella Larsen: *Quicksand & Passing* (Serpent's Tail, London 1989)
James McBride: *The Color of Water* (Bloomsbury, London 1998)
May Opitz, Katharina Oguntoye & Dagmar Schultz: *Showing Our Colors* (University of Massachusetts Press 1992)
John P. Parker: *Autobiography* (W. W. Norton, New York 1996)
Maria P. P. Root: *The Multiracial Experience: Racial Borders as the New Frontier* (Sage Publications, California 1996)
Paul Rosenblatt, Terri A. Karis & Richard D. Powell: *Multiracial Couples: Black & White Voices* (Sage Publications, California 1995)
Leone Ross: *All the Blood is Red* (Angela Royal Publishing, London 1996)
Lucinda Roy: *Lady Moses* (Virago, London 1998)
Mary Seacole: *Wonderful Adventures of Mrs Seacole in Many Lands* (Falling Wall Press, Bristol 1984)
Jon Michael Spencer: *The New Colored People: The Mixed-Race Movement in America* (New York University Press 1997)
Paul R. Spickard: *Mixed Blood* (University of Wisconsin Press 1989)
Stuart Seely Sprague (ed.): *His Promised Land: The Autobiography of John P. Parker* (W. W. Norton, New York 1996)
Kathryn Talalay: *Composition in Black and White: The Life of Philippa Schuyler* (Oxford University Press 1995)
Barbara Tizard & Ann Phoenix: *Black, White or Mixed Race?* (Routledge, London 1993)
Phil Vasili: *Arthur Wharton 1865-1930* (Frank Cass, London 1998)
Alex Wheatle: *Brixton Rock* (BlackAmber Books, London 1999)
Robert Wedderburn: *The Horrors of Slavery and Other Writings* (Edinburgh University Press, Edinburgh 1991)
Naomi Zack (ed.): *American Mixed Race* (Rowman & Littlefield, London 1995)

Children's Books

Rachel Anderson: *Princess Jazz and the Angels* (Mammoth, London 1995)
Shango Baku: *Beacons of Liberation: Twelve Black Leaders* (CETTIE, London 1995)
Tony Bradman & Eileen Browne: *Through My Window* (Mammoth, London 1989)

Tony Bradman & Eileen Browne: *Wait and See* (Mammoth, London 1990)

Tony Bradman & Eileen Browne: *In a Minute* (Mammoth, London 1991)

David W. Bygott: *Black and British* (Oxford University Press, Oxford 1992)

Sean Dolan: *Bob Marley* (Chelsea House, New York 1997)

Vivian French: *Zenobia and Mouse* (Walker, London 1990)

Sarah Garland: *Billy and Belle* (Puffin, London 1993)

Zerbanoo Gifford: *Asian Presence in Europe* (Mantra, London 1995)

Carlotta Hacker: *Great African Americans in History* (Crabtree, New York 1997)

Wade Hudson & Valerie Wilson Wesley: *Book of Black Heroes Vol 1* (Just Us Books, Orange NJ 1988)

Toyomi Igus et al: *Book of Black Heroes Vol 2: Great Women in the Struggle* (Just Us Books, Orange NJ 1991)

Catherine Johnson: *Other Colours* (The Women's Press, London 1997)

Bethany Kandel: *Trevor's Story: Growing Up Biracial* (Lerner Publications, Minneapolis 1997)

Deborah King: *Pride of Black British Women* (Hansib, London 1995)

Liverpool Race Equality Team: *John Archer* (Liverpool City Council 1995)

Jocelyn Emama Maxime: *Black Like Me: Mixed Parentage* (Emani Publications, London 1994)

Beverley Naidoo: *Letang and Julie Save the Day* (Longman, Harlow 1994)

Beverley Naidoo: *Letang's New Friend* (Longman, Harlow 1994)

Jennifer Northway: *Lucy's Day Trip* (Mammoth, London 1992)

Jennifer Northway: *Lucy's Rabbit* (Scholastic, London 1995)

Jennifer Northway: *Lucy's Quarrel* (Scholastic, London 1997)

Philip Pullman: *The Broken Bridge* (Macmillan, London 1990)

David Rhys: *Where's Gran* (Tamarind, Camberley nd)

Sharman Apt Russell: *Frederick Douglass* (Chelsea House, New York 1998)

Alan Schroeder: *Booker T. Washington* (Chelsea House, New York 1992)

Jessica Souhami: *Mother Caught a Flea* (Frances Lincoln, London 1998)

Jessica Souhami: *One Potato, Two Potato* (Frances Lincoln, London 1998)

Verna Allette Wilkins: *Boots for a Bridesmaid* (Tamarind, Camberley 1995)

Sharon Dennis Wyeth: *The World of Daughter McGuire* (Bantam Doubleday Dell, New York 1994)

SUPPORT GROUPS

People in Harmony, 49 Ledgers Road, Slough, Berks SL1 2RQ, Tel: 01753 552 559

Mosaic, Community Base, 113-117 Queen's Road, Brighton, East Sussex BN1 3XG, Tel: 01273 234 107

Black Child Mixed Parentage, 1 Mole Place, Oxford, Oxon OX4 5SD, Tel: 01865 396 611

Dimali, African/Caribbean Project, 2 Bath Place, Leamington Spa, Warwickshire, CV31 3AQ

Unity, Fulford Family Centre, 237-239 Gatehouse Avenue, Withywood, Bristol BS13 9AQ, Tel: 0117 978 2441

The Harmony Project, 372 Newhampton Road, Whitmore Reans, Wolverhampton, WV6 0RX, Tel: 01902 421 783